It Has Always Been You

THE POWER OF UNDERSTANDING YOUR WORTH

SLOAN KOESTER

This book is dedicated to the beautiful people who continuously build me up and support me—the ones who love me regardless of the amount of sass and stubbornness I dish out daily. To my best friends and my family, I love you dearly and am beyond thankful for your impact on my life. I look forward to every new experience and adventure with you because this is only the beginning.

A special thank you to my dad, who has always helped me achieve my dreams. Anything that I set my mind to he supports undoubtedly and wholeheartedly, finding every possible way for it to be accomplished. I love you, Dad, and I'm so lucky I get to be your mini-me. Koester and Koester forever!

A special thank you to my mom, who has introduced me to cultures of all kinds since I was born. You taught me about different religions, languages, foods, and countries, handed me a book to read every time I had a question, and let my mind wander until I found the path that was right for me. I love you, Mom. Thank you for my endless back scratches, Nora Jones songs, and for teaching me the importance of bubble baths, Harry Potter, and empathy.

Contents

Preface

This book is interesting for quite a few reasons. It's filled with different ideas I have, my love for international affairs and other cultures, and my views on the world. It's a compilation of the world through my eyes and interests. It takes you on a journey of my own personal growth and change. It brings to life the advice I follow for myself and how I continue to grow as a person. No one is perfect, and in a world where perfection and flawlessness are portrayed all over social media and television, I hope this book gives you a breath of fresh air. I want it to take you on an experience of love, adventure, and self-exploration. I hope that it sparks inspiration and excitement and pushes you to try new things, reevaluate your life situation, and open the door for new opportunities. This life is for everyone, and every single person should get the chance to be showered in happiness, support, and love.

My Hope for You

I hope this book becomes a tool you can always turn to when you're feeling off, struggling with hard decisions, need to find yourself again, or need a refresher on embracing your worth and capability. I made it small so it can be taken with you on any kind of journey, and it can fit perfectly on a bedside table, providing a constant reminder that you are enough every single day. I think of this book as something that you can keep if you need it, or you can pass it on to someone else who might benefit. Not everyone will need these ideas, advice, or realizations, but the thought of not having them out there for someone who does was my motivation in creating it.

CHAPTER 1

Paving Your Way Through Life

Life is filled with many obstacles. It challenges us daily, forces us to push ourselves, and makes exceptions for no one. As you travel through life, it's important to remember your growth— the experiences and chapters that you've lived through. Everything we do becomes a piece of us. Everything that happens to us shapes us. Each day we are creating our path of life. Individual days may not always seem important. They may seem like just another day at the office, another day of school, chores, and mundane tasks. Yet, what we do each day is what creates who we are. These days strung together eventually become the story of your life. These are the moments you look back on and the times you cherish. They'll be filled with the people who helped shape you throughout your time on Earth. Actively choosing how you'll spend your twenty-four hours gives you the power to make the day yours. You are the leader of your life, you are in charge of your decisions, and you are capable of accomplishing every fantastic thing you want to in this world.

Once you start to realize the importance each day holds, your world will change. It's so powerful to wake up each morning knowing it's another beautiful chance to learn, create, love, and embrace whatever comes your way. As I look back, I realize I've wasted far too many days feeling sorry for myself, blaming myself, being upset with situations out of my control, and being bothered with others. Once I became conscious of the fact that I'm in charge of how I feel and how I handle situations, I felt like a massive weight had been lifted off me.

You don't need to run your own company to be your own boss. You have always been in charge of yourself. If you don't feel you hold this power, think about what you can adjust in your life to find it. It may require some uncomfortable conversations, the removal of toxic relationships, or a change in scenery, but whatever you need to do to claim your power, may you never forget it has always been within you. You have always been enough. You hold incredible value, and I hope you never feel as if you take up too much space. There's no one else like you, and I want you to take up space. I want you to grow, heal, and flourish into the person you are meant to be.

I remember being in high school and the littlest things seemed like my whole world. One fight with my boyfriend and game over—the world is ending. If my mom wouldn't drop me off at my friend's house—everything is ruined. I'm the only one who can't hang out, so I'm going to just cry in my room all day. I failed my driver's test five times—I'll never be able to drive. The man at the DMV kindly told me that if I failed it one more time, I wouldn't be able to try again until I was eighteen. When I went for the sixth time, I missed my number being called, and of course, I started crying. The drama was too much to handle, so I simply went home. High school was filled with so many emotions, changes, and life decisions. I realized when I got to college that I had to tone it down. Who has time to always be so upset about minor inconveniences or life situations? I would let my emotions consume me, and I would let the energy of everyone around fill me. It was beyond draining. Yet, it took me three years into college to really make some profound changes. Why did it take me so long? I didn't understand myself. I had spent so much time focused on other people that I never took the time to get to know myself, to love myself, or to understand myself. I started being dedicated to myself for the first time ever. I started focusing on my needs, my happiness, and my life goals. I decided that no matter where I went or what happened, I would never let myself feel empty or alone because I would always have myself. I began removing people from my life who didn't align with my goals, who didn't support me, and who used me. This created a healthy space for me to grow and embrace myself.

Each day we journey through becomes a piece of the story of our lives. You have the power to make yourself a priority and to surround yourself with those who align with you. You have the ability to remove anything that no longer serves you.

It's crucial that we give ourselves the love we give others. It's important that we value ourselves, that we care for ourselves, and that we hold ourselves up. The key to realizing your full potential has always been within you. It's up to you to unlock it. It's up to you to create positive change in your life and learn how to love with yourself. You are the most fantastic person, and there is only one you in the world. How crazy is that? The way you smile, the way you view the world, the way you love, the way you speak—it's all unique to you. When I really grasped this concept, I was fully convinced that I was the most extraordinary person on the planet. I felt like Superman—all ready to save the day and such.

Life is quite complex, as many of us have come to know. It comes at you fast, and at times it can feel like you're just going through the motions. You're trying to stay afloat and understand the complexity. You may have feel confused about whether you've made the right choices, feel like you don't belong, or feel alone. No one walks through life making all the right moves, questioning their situations or choices. Social media plays a significant role in how we view the world. It's as if we switch from reality to fantasy. It's a confusing and unhealthy mix that drives our confusion and false perceptions of the world even further.

Emotions, for example, are entirely normal. They're not only normal, they're essential and powerful tools. They allow you to feel the world around you. They give you guiding hints through your experiences. Emotions offer you cues about the people you're close with, the people you don't know, and the environment that surrounds you. I used to think that my emotions were a burden. My physical and mental reactions consumed me at times. When I was sixteen and cried over my boyfriend or missing out on social situations, I wasn't conscious of the impact that feeling things so strongly had on me. It had both a psychological and physical effect. I would feel confused, angry, sad, and hurt, but I would also feel shaky, lose my appetite, and have insomnia. I hated emotions back then because I was unable to control them. They took me over completely, and sometimes they put me at very low places, but I would still not change any of that learning, experience, or growth.

As my life became filled with more commitments, college, work, and internships, I began to get tired of my emotions consuming me. I still am and will forever be learning about myself, growing, healing, and finding ways to fill my life with happiness and love. I refuse to give myself anything less. I still struggle with my emotions, but now I'm consciously aware of them, how they make me feel, how to choose my reaction, how to pick myself up again, and how to view my situations in a different light. I became fed up with my emotions because sometimes they made my days feel extra heavy, and they made it hard to be productive, retain information, and make the most out of my experiences. I decided to start by listening to my body and not forcing myself into situations where I didn't feel comfortable. In college, I would force myself to do the things everyone else liked, to be around the people everyone raved about. Yet, I was often left feeling sad, empty, and confused. It had me questioning myself. It had me wondering why I didn't fit into the same scenes as others and how the things that seemed to fulfil others did not fulfil me. Though sadness, hurt, and confusion washed over me, I began to be thankful for my emotions. I didn't want to be around people who made me question myself, my values, and my abilities. Who would?

Sometimes we spend so much time, energy, and effort to fit in to the world around us that we forget the beauty in being true to ourselves. We forget how important it is to respect ourselves and stick up for ourselves. As I began falling in love with my studies and removing the negativity from my life, I was quickly filled with large amounts of gratitude.

This alone allowed me to have far more positive moments with myself. I was able to devote more time to myself, my studies, and doing the things I loved. When people or situations interfered with that, I made note of it. I made note of how it made me feel. Going into university, I had difficulty saying no because I genuinely felt obligated to say yes. It's very odd to feel like you need to say yes to everyone. You don't owe anyone anything. That's the bottom line. No one is entitled to your space, time, energy, love, or money. Once I began to say no, friendships began to die; people stopped asking me for things because they realized I would not simply fall into the trap of saying yes. Interestingly, I had rarely asked these people for anything. When I did, they had no problem saying no to me. It didn't matter if I wanted company to eat with or if I needed a ride in the pouring rain; these people were always unavailable. They constantly made excuses, and I never picked up on it. But once I started saying no, the game changed entirely. I found myself having even more time to learn about myself, spend time in school, focus on my goals, and spend time with the people I loved.

Sometimes the people who are closest to us can be the ones putting us down. When evaluating your emotions and circumstances, I encourage you to break down your current relationships. Make a pros and cons list, take note of how these people make you feel, if your relationship has changed, and why that might be. Look at the people in your circle and honestly evaluate them. Remember that your circle of people should feel like sunshine in your life; they should make the bad days good and the good days better. They should not stand in your way or block your light. They should empower you and be proud of you. They should love you fully and embrace your uniqueness. They should recognize that you are and will always be one of a kind. You're not asking too much. This is when you begin to embrace the energy, love, and care that you deserve.

Removing toxicity from your life creates space to attract new energy and people. It also gives you time to grow as a person and redefine your values, standards, and goals. I find myself readjusting quite frequently. To me, it's very beneficial. When I encounter emotions that I don't enjoy feeling, I readjust. If I realize I don't like studying a particular topic; I readjust. If I intern at a company and recognize that the specific field is not for me; I readjust. Every time we readjust, we align ourselves with the correct path. I will be readjusting in different areas of my life for the rest of my time on Earth. It's required for growth, perception, and self-love. Respect yourself enough to not force yourself into things you don't enjoy. You have nothing to prove to anyone. You don't need anyone else's light; you are your own beautiful light. You're not on this Earth to be like everyone else or to fall for the false social media reality. You're here to be you, to do the things you want to do, and to accomplish every dream you have.

Life moves quickly, which can have both a positive and negative impact on us. The good news is that a bad day is only twenty-four hours. The bad news is that the good moments do not last forever, even though we wish they would. As I got older, I started to truly value the people in my circle—the people who filled me with love on even the hardest days. I began to realize my parents were growing older and that they were the same as me—humans navigating through life to the best of their ability. I remember one of my mentors telling me to find the people who would be there for me in the worst times of my life. I sat with that idea for a second, but it didn't quite sink in. She went on to say, "I have been there for my friends through divorce, death, miscarriages, job losses, and more." She expressed how the good parts of friendships and celebrations are nothing short of excellent, but the bad times in life call for the truest of friends. The people who would do anything to make sure you're okay. The people who become family. The ones you can cry on and show yourself at rock bottom to. The bad times call for genuine kindness and support. You deserve this level of support and love. If you feel alone and feel as if you don't have this support system, I'm here to tell you that you do. It has always been within you. You have always been enough. You are strong, you are worthy of happiness, and you are capable of beautiful friendships and relationships. It's never too late to begin again. It's never too late to seek out these friendships. Wherever you are on this planet, find people who align with you. Create a routine that helps you feel at home. I personally enjoy shopping at the same places, seeing familiar faces, and feeling welcomed. I enjoy surrounding myself with like-minded people with shared interests. This could be a book club, an after-work gaming group, or a workout buddy—I urge you to find something like this and stick to it. As silly as it may sound, the fact that the checkout people at Trader Joe's know my name and ask me how I'm doing makes me feel at home. Going to Orangetheory classes, where my coach knows my name, and seeing familiar, smiling faces makes me very happy. The people I have met during my time at Florida State so far have made a new city feel like home. They've made a program I had never studied feel like I was meant for it. The sense of community when you begin to align yourself with your values, dreams, and life aspirations is a beautiful thing. It's not easy, and some days aren't as great as others, but that is growth. We are constantly taking in the world around us and creating our path of life. Every day we create the life we want to tell our grandchildren about, write a book about, or feel completely fulfilled by and alive in. The reality is that regardless of money, circumstances, and age, most everyone craves love and a life they are proud of. It's okay to struggle; in fact, it's necessary for growth. We all have different struggles, but the idea still applies to us all. When we're put into new, uncomfortable situations, we grow. When we begin a journey alone, whether it be divorce, death, or other reasons, we grow. I think the most challenging concept for me to grasp was that we don't ask for this type of growth. It's usually thrown at us full speed, and we slowly learn to pick up the pieces and make sense of what's happening. Regardless, we continue. We continue on this path of life to see the beautiful light that illuminates the end of the tunnel. We live for the good moments, which will hopefully outnumber the bad. As our perceptions change and our views on the world shifts, the wounds that once hurt us so deeply, the cries for help, are finally healed. I envision gardens growing in all the parts of me that have been damaged. Delicate flowers fill the space with pastel colors, closing the wounds that once were. It makes me feel powerful to know the things I can overcome. Our minds and bodies are resilient—they can push through far more than we can imagine. If you're at a time in your life where you feel broken and empty, envision the flowers growing in your wounds. Envision your wondrous garden of beauty, the colors filling you, and the stems sealing every inch of your pain like stitches gifted from nature. Take some time to thank your body and mind for their resilience. Give yourself a big hug and know that you have gardens within you and love flowing throughout you. It has always been you.

As we navigate through life, it's vital that we recognize our worth and understand our value. These tools allow you to continue your path of life while realigning and refusing anything but the best for yourself. The best is what you deserve. It can be hard at times; you may get fired, broken up with, fail a class, or keep people around who aren't deserving of you because you don't want to be lonely. This is normal, and this is life. What's important is that you learn to recognize these patterns, and you realize that even when these life events happen, your worth does not decrease. Think of your life as a puzzle; if you get fired from a job, the world doesn't take one of your pieces. If fact, you gain another piece. Your puzzle continues to grow just like you do. Your worth inevitably increases. Your puzzle continues to gain pieces over time until it is solidified together as the story of you. We are not made of the things that happen to us; we are made of how we react, how we survive, and how we overcome and heal.

WE ARE ONLY HUMAN

As we navigate through life, we transition through many stages. We grow, we change, we adapt, we hurt, we feel, and we continue. We all need to understand one essential thing—life is not easy. I'm sure most of us know this by now. I'm sure you have been through things you may not talk about or fully understand, and that's okay. As we grow up and graduate high school, college, or find ourselves going straight into the workforce, we start to see the world through a different lens. Life can be full of long days. It can feel tiring and, at times, mundane. What I hope we all find as we grow is the unique opportunities that life has to offer us. I hope you find your "why" in life and your purpose because, whether you believe it or not, you do have one. I hope you find your place in life and work hard doing so. You're deserving of great opportunities, love, happiness, and a great life. I hope that I'm creating my path to success and my place in this world. However, success is different for everyone, and there are many kinds of success. Some of my ideas of success are:

- Doing what I love and doing it phenomenally well
- Being financially comfortable
- Having a healthy and strong body
- Loving myself through all my phases
- Being truly happy

We're all going through this journey with different hurdles and obstacles in our way. Social media is fake and creates a false reality. Become your biggest supporter and best friend. You're the person you will always have in your life, so love yourself endlessly. Life is hard, and it takes time, determination, and dedication to get to where you want to be. Stop comparing your journey to the journeys of those around you and fall in love with your own. Some things I do to better myself and find peace in my life are Orangetheory Fitness, yoga, reading, sunset walks, writing, and playing with animals.

At the end of the day, we are only human. We can only do so much, and we can only push ourselves so far. You are loved, and you are worthy of all good things. Make taking care of yourself a top priority and learn to understand both your personal limits and those in the world around you.

SHOWERED IN GRATITUDE

I want to thank you for being here and being a part of this beautiful ride. Writing has always been a passion of mine, and now that I've been writing for over a year, it has become an integral part of my life. I'm thankful for your presence and for every time you choose to pick up this book or read any of my work.

Recently, everything about life has made me smile. Sometimes, I let myself get in my head and think of the negative or sad aspects, but recently, I've realized how incredible life is. As I sit at my desk writing, I catch a glimpse of the sun shining over the buildings before it tucks away for the night, letting me know that I have completed another day and am ready to rest for the next. I've also fallen so deeply in love with mornings; every single one of them. Whether it's the early gray skies with rain tiptoeing against my window or the radiant light that shines through my curtains, letting me know it's time to rise, I love it all. I love the meaning of my mornings and the time I get to spend alone, practicing gratitude, happiness, and preparing myself for another day.

I love peeking out my window to see the busy street and blue skies throughout the day, but I also love the stormy days that let me know it's okay to relax and find happiness even on darker days. I'm thankful for myself, the growth I have had, and the growth I continue to push for. Some days set me back, but in the long run, they move me so much farther forward.

I'm thankful for my days spent studying and the amount of knowledge I'm lucky enough to gain. I'm grateful for the kind smiles and friendly gestures I experience throughout the day, even if it's all done by strangers. I'm thankful for my friends who make anywhere feel like home. I'm grateful for my experiences. Both the good and the bad have all shaped me into the person I am today.

I'm thankful for my ability to write and relay

empowerment to others. I'm filled with joy that I can love those around me and show them their strengths and potential. I'm thankful for this wonderful life, even on the days when I question the purpose of it all. Life is an intricate mix of complicated and beautiful. Each day brings new adventures or hardships. Each day brings things no one could possibly predict or understand. Life is complex, but it's a journey I wouldn't trade for anything. It's a journey I'm forever grateful for, and one I will continuously learn from.

As you continue to create your own life, I hope you find what is meaningful to you and the importance of pursuing your dreams. No one is here by accident, and even though the code to life's mysterious ways will never be cracked, we can still enjoy the complexity and find grace throughout the journey. You have the freedom to choose how you feel about the world, how you perceive the world, and what choices you'll make next. You are in control. Take hold of the reigns, take hold of your power—everything you need to succeed has always been within you.

CHAPTER 2

Understanding the World Around You

The world is a complex place that we sail through daily. We strive to make sense of it all, even during the roughest times. Some moments in life are intriguing to me. For instance, one day, my schoolwork may seem like the most important thing on the planet, and another day, I find myself staring out a plane window and realizing we live on a floating rock. There's usually no in-between for me. It's really crazy how so many things are going on in the world, yet we're still here living our day-to-day lives. Realizing this has helped me put things into perspective and make time for what I love. There is no guarantee that we have another day on Earth, so making the most of today is the go-to move. For me, traveling is a great way to live in the moment and make the most of my time. In December 2021, I traveled alone to Antigua, Guatemala, for a month to do Spanish immersion. I met the most beautiful people, inside and out. Traveling helps me see the world through a different lens and learn about other people and cultures. One of my passions is learning about languages because it's so necessary to relating to and understanding other people.

I find the greatest joy in learning other languages and being able to communicate with those around me. The biggest smile comes across my face when I realize I can express my needs and feelings and don't need English to accomplish it. Hearing other languages around me is like music to my ears and brings such happiness to my soul. These next few stories will give you a glimpse into my time in Guatemala.

ANTIGUA, GUATEMALA

I Am on My Way, December 2021

Getting ready for Guatemala was an interesting experience, to say the least. I had no idea what to bring. I had my carry-on black suitcase and olive-green North Face backpack to stuff with enough to last me approximately one month. Coming from Florida, where the norm is wearing swimsuits that cover about as much skin as a thong from Victoria's Secret, and going to school in Tallahassee, where tops covered half your breast if you were lucky and shorts had ass cheeks hanging out of them, I wasn't sure I was equipped with the proper clothing. In the end, I packed about five outfits—jeans with no holes, leggings, t-shirts, one zip-up jacket, and three pairs of shoes. I had to get my covid test before I left, and I was so nervous that I took three tests just to make sure none of them were too old.

The lady at Walgreens, where I did drive-thru covid tests, began to recognize me and give me odd looks. I shouted out of the car window, "I'm going to Guatemala! I just want to make sure I don't have covid!" It turned out that my saying I'm going to Guatemala made people look at me even more peculiarly.

My flight took off at 6:00 am the day I left. Waiting in line to show security my passport, I felt so nervous. What on Earth was I doing? The man grabbed my passport, stared at me, stared at me some more, and said, "Guatemala City?" I did a nervous laugh and said, "Yup! Going to learn Spanish!" He raised his eyebrow, handed back my passport, and yelled, "Next!"

I had a connection in Atlanta; fast and easy it went. Now I had arrived at my gate for Guatemala City. The international terminal is always my favorite terminal in every airport. It's like heaven to me. I see all these places, and I want to jump on the planes and go, go, go. It sends a little fire through my belly, and I feel this need to explore the entire planet.

As I sat at my gate, everyone around me was speaking Spanish. I was so excited I could have screamed with happiness. I started to get some looks as we boarded, and I had friends and family members trying to call me and wish me luck and get updates, but no. The last thing I was going to do was blow my cover by not speaking Spanish, so I simply kept my mouth closed. As I boarded the plane, personal space became a thing of the past. Between loud calls to relatives, bursts of laughter, guitars flying over my head in every direction, and no English, I was convinced I was in the movie Coco. Still trying not to blow my cover, I put the setting on my TV to French. Everything was going well until we ordered our food. The flight attendant looked at the man next to me, spoke Spanish to him, and then looked at me and spoke English. I was pissed. Cover blown. I looked at him with a stern face and said, "I'll have the grain bowl, thank you."

When I and what felt like five hundred guitars got off the plane, I began to go through immigration. Two white men with beer bellies and Chaco sandals were in front of me in line. The two girls running the line looked at them and said something in Spanish. "Um, can you speak English?" one rudely said. The girls just looked at them. Embarrassed and knowing they were, of course, from my country, I said, "We are going through immigration, so get out your passport, vaccine card, and fill out your sheet. It's not that difficult." The man let out an "oh okay, thanks" and walked ahead. As I went to find my luggage, there were what felt like a million carousels filled with suitcases and hundreds of families running around. I remember being told before I left that there were boys who would help me take my luggage off the carousel if I paid them. Of course, I didn't have any cash yet, so that wasn't an option. One hour and one panic attack later, I found my bag. One of the men was pointing at it, trying to get it for me, but since I had no cash and didn't want to hurt his feelings, I ran up to where he was pointing and ripped my bag right off the carousel. He did a confused laugh and looked at me like I had five heads. There was no time to explain, so I waved, smiled, and ran off to go through customs. The line was so long, longer than I had ever seen before in any airport. I stood there for what felt like hours, but I finally made it through.

I went to leave the airport, and it was as if everyone and their mother were crowding the doorway. I was supposed to look for a man holding a yellow smiley face flag. How on Earth would I be able to find it? Soon enough, I saw it waving amid all the commotion. When I reached him, he asked in Spanish if I spoke Spanish, and I responded with a guilty no. We walked toward the car lot, and I was able to make out with my limited understanding of Spanish that he was going to go get the car. He left to go get it, and I wished I knew enough Spanish to say, "Take me with you to the car, please!" Instead, I stood alone on the sidewalk and waited. As crowds of people walked past me, I didn't want to come across as alone or weak and certainly didn't want to seem as lost as I was. So I practiced my pissed-off faces, some fighting moves in my head, started speaking French to the air around me, and smiling and waving at strangers so maybe they would think I fit in. Soon enough, the car pulled up, which was quite a relief because the show I was putting on was getting very old. He drove me to my host mom's house, handed me my luggage, led me inside, and left. My host mom looked at me and said, "Hablas español?" to which I responded no. She nodded her head and continued in Spanish, showing me how to use my key, work the shower and toilet, and what time dinner was.

The next day, my roommate arrived. She came right after our dinner. She had come from Costa Rica. Her suitcase was zip-tied shut, and we could not get it open for the life of us. I used my Google Translate to find out what *scissors* and *knife* were in Spanish and asked my host mom for some *cuchillos y tijeras*. She handed them to me and then followed me to my room with a concerned look on her face. As we sat on the floor trying to open the suitcase, my host mom began to laugh, probably thankful we weren't up to any trouble. That night, my roommate, Ruthie, talked in her sleep. It had to have been around one in the morning, and we both had school the next morning. "What the hell are we doing here?" she said as she sat up. Jolted out of sleep and not knowing the answer to her question, I just stared at her. She then just fell back asleep, and so did I. *Welcome to Guatemala*! I thought.

THE BEGINNING

I'm so happy.

I don't know how, but I feel so at home. I feel more comfortable here than I did on my first day of college in South Carolina or Florida. It's weird how somewhere so different can feel like home. How people who do not speak your language still understand you, and how people are so welcoming even when you feel like you're so different.

I love the warm smiles, waves, and *buenos días* greetings as I walk to school in the morning. I love my Spanish classes and the interesting people I get to meet every day. I love every part of it, and it fills me with so much gratitude.

Before this trip, many of my friends and family discussed only the dangers and risks of the journey. It definitely scared me, but not enough to cancel the trip.

Being with people who are different than me and learning new cultures and languages will always be my passion. It fills my soul with happiness and makes me feel so alive. This is the life I want to remember, and these are the memories I want to have forever.

I've made so many new friends already and continue to share laughs, meals, and wonderful conversations with the most amazing people. I've already taken a cooking class at my school and look forward to my weekly salsa classes and more cooking classes.

I'm proud of myself for always following my heart and staying true to my passions. I'm thankful for my independence and drive to create positive change.

The town of Antigua is filled with beautiful stone-covered roads and buildings that look like a pack of Skittles. It's heavenly. I love the early mornings—the air is crisp and a little chilly, the birds are chirping, and the mountains sit high and mighty with clouds hanging over the tops. I'm extra thankful for life right now and the wonderful people I have in it.

Te amo mucho, Guatemala.

TE EXTRAÑO, GUATEMALA

Oh, how much I miss you, Guatemala. I tell everyone about you, and when I shut my eyes and go to my happy place, it's you that I see. I really miss the big smiles, warm gestures, and friends I had when I was with you. I miss the Spanish rolling off my tongue and being able to walk every inch of you with a smile, so everyone could feel my happiness. I miss my host family, I miss our meals, and I miss my best friends that I made with you. You made me feel so at home, your people are so kind, your culture is so beautiful, and I will find time to come back to my new home away from home. You came at a time in my life when I was ready for adventure but also a bit lost. You pushed my limits, for I did not know your language when I arrived, but you made me fall in love with it in a matter of hours, and for that, I'm forever thankful.

COMING BACK TO THE STATES

Before leaving Antigua, I felt a small twinge of homesickness or restlessness; I'm not sure which. I felt like I had run away to a new country for a month and was now in this in-between phase of "I am doing something really cool" and "I am doing nothing at all." As the cab driver picked me up to take me back to Guatemala City, his kind eyes looked back in the mirror and asked me, "*¿Cómo fue tu tiempo en Guatemala?*" I responded, "*Me encanta estar aquí, me entristece irme.*" As tears began to fill my eyes and the van drove across the bumpy roads leaving Antigua, I realized how sad I was to leave. The news had been constantly updating about the pandemic raging in America and everything going on in the world, and I felt as if I were leaving my safe space and going back to reality.

When I got back to Tallahassee, still sad about leaving

my colorful little oasis, a weird thing happened. It was as if I had gotten culture shock coming back to my own country. The streets seemed so empty every day; the buildings so modern, edgy, and bulky; and no one smiled at me. In fact, it seemed that people just stared at me and walked away, or groups of people would laugh and run by me. Oh, how desperately I wanted to go back. I wanted the warm smiles, the friendly greetings, and feeling of being part of the society. Now I felt like a lone person just wandering. Dinner was no longer made as a family and served at a table full of my friends. I now had to find time to eat, which was usually a fast meal because of my school workload, and I almost always ate alone. As time went by, I adjusted back to the ways of American society, but took me a couple of months. Now when I close my eyes and think of where I am happiest, I go to the colorful streets filled with smiles, children, laughter, and mopeds of Antigua, Guatemala.

THE POWER OF TRAVELING ALONE

The power of traveling alone is endless. It helps you find your individuality and explore aspects of yourself that you haven't before. It pushes you out of your comfort zone, it breaks your assumptions about a place, and it surrounds you with culture, beautiful people, wonderful adventures, and growth. Traveling alone can be scary, exhilarating, and emotional. It continuously pushes me to explore myself and my surroundings. It gives me the chance to make connections with people from all over the world.

I enjoy immersing myself in new cultures and testing my limits. It provides me with a healthy push to grow as a person and equips me to make positive changes in the world. Something that is extremely important to me is to try to understand other people. I love to make people feel heard, loved, accepted, and happy. Language plays a large role in this, which is why I strive to learn as much as I can. I want to be able to connect with people and understand them.

I loved walking along the cobblestone roads and taking in the fresh air as I went to school, to a cafe, or home. It filled me with happiness and gratitude to know I was experiencing such a lovely place. I'm very thankful for my trip to Antigua, Guatemala, and I will surely go back. The people are so inviting, kind, and warm that it fills my heart. I'm grateful I get to feel so at home in a place so different than my own.

I urge you to try travelling alone. It can be scary, but staying the same is even scarier. Push yourself to understand those who are different than you and embrace the beauty of uniqueness that other places and people can offer you.

Always remember that you are strong, you are capable, you are smart, and you are aware.

ACATENANGO

When I first arrived at school in Antigua, I met a girl from Amsterdam. After our orientation, she began talking to me about an epic hike called Acatenango. "It makes your legs shake, it's so hard, the elevation is crazy, and I can't wait to do it!" she said with so much excitement. I thought, *You know, I really don't think that's a Sloan-friendly activity.* I like the outdoors, of course, but this seemed to push the limits.

I met my roommate the next day, and we started to think of excursions we wanted to do while we were there. "Acatenango—we have to do it!" she said. I was still very hesitant. Everyone had been telling me how hard it was; many people said it was the hardest thing they had ever done.

I thought, *There's no way I go up that volcano.*

Well, sure enough, after school one day, my roommate and I headed over to the travel agency, and there were two spots left. We would be hiking the volcano on Christmas Eve and Christmas Day. I was scared, to say the least, but anyone who knows me knows I will be the first to take the leap and dive in headfirst.

The next morning, we waited for the bus to pick us up. I was half-hoping they would forget about us, but of course the bus pulled up, and off we went. We were taken to a building where we checked in, rented backpacks, and were supplied with our meals and equipment. We loaded up in the bus and began the hour-long journey to Acatenango.

Anxious but filled with excitement, we gathered at the base of the volcano.

The first two hours were the worst. As I climbed up the rocky volcano with dust swirling in the air, I felt my heart beating in my chest, ears, and head. The sweat dripped down my body, and breathing easily became a thing of the past. It was an uncomfortable feeling. With every step up, I slid three steps back. I wanted so badly to give up. The packs I carried on both my back and front felt so heavy as I trekked up the slippery volcano. I wondered what the hell I had gotten myself into. The sun beat down on my face for what felt like an eternity, and then suddenly, it didn't. The once pale, rocky, slippery terrain became dark and shaded with greenery all around. A cool breeze blew against me, and we finally stopped for lunch.

We ate garlic bread that was toasted over the fire and warm pasta with homemade sauce. It was *amazing*. It started to get a little chilly; the group began to add some layers and get ready for the next three to four hours of our uphill battle. As we climbed, I had moments of feeling both strong and weak, but I was still going up. The views were stunning. The temperature started to drop drastically, and my hands felt cold and sore around my walking stick, but we finally made it. A feeling of relief washed over me when we got to the campsite. We dropped our bags off in our tent and headed over to the fire with everyone. The views from the campsite were something I had never experienced before. Being so high up, away from society, and gazing across the horizon was life changing. Joy radiated all around us, and the warmth of the fire filled me with peace. Effortless conversations floated around the campfire, and the sounds of laughter spread among the group.

We watched the sun slowly fade away and pastel colors painted the sky. The darkness of night began to descend, and the rumbles from the Fuego volcano began. Sitting down for Christmas dinner, singing songs, and enjoying one another's company, I felt very at home—even at the top of a volcano.

The next morning, I woke up and unzipped the tent door to a beautiful sunrise. The chilly air woke me up and began to prepare me for the trek down. Everyone shared a wonderful breakfast, packed up, and began to tackle the adventure down.

I was convinced that there was no way going down

would be harder, but I quickly realized I was mistaken. Going down was just as hard but in a completely different way. I slid for about three hours, and many times felt as if I was skiing in my sneakers. My legs were shaking and my knees were throbbing as I tried not to faceplant or break my back. Watching others in my group run or slip down the mountain reminded me that I needed to seriously focus, or I could get very hurt. When we arrived at the bottom, my body was filled with exhaustion but so relieved to be finished. I'm so thankful for the amazing group I went with and the company I booked through. Here are some tips if you want to take this amazing hike:

What you should know:

- Bring altitude sickness pills.

- Bring pain relievers. Headaches and body aches are very common in high altitudes.

- Hiking boots are best (My gym shoes barely cut it).

- Bring layers; it gets very cold.

- You can bring extra cash to pay for a porter (a person to carry your bags up).

- Rent a walking stick or two (you can rent them at the base of the volcano).

- It can feel harder to breathe in higher altitudes, so take it easy until your body adjusts.

Overall, it was such an amazing experience, and I'm beyond thankful I was able to be a part of it. It's absolutely the hardest hike I've ever done, but that just makes the experience even better.

Thank you, Acatenango.

My time spent in Guatemala was filled with the most caring people, and I loved nothing more than the friendly faces that filled the beautiful cobblestone streets. I loved learning Spanish and feeling so excited to be able to communicate with others. The relationships and emotions I felt during my time there were almost indescribable. Traveling alone is such an amazing experience. I gained so much knowledge about another place on Earth, but I believe I learned the most about myself and who I am as a person. Travelling alone pushes you out of your comfort zone and forces you to experience things you normally would not. I learned that many things I was told about Guatemala before I traveled there were wildly inaccurate. I've experienced this disconnect between perception and reality when I traveled to other countries as well. When you see things with your own eyes, it completely changes your perspective on the world. I'm so thankful for my decision to travel solo in Guatemala despite the pandemic and false information I received before going. Sending love to my host family, my teachers at school, my roommate, and all the wonderful people I shared meals with throughout my time there.

You've made an indelible positive impact on me, and I'm forever grateful for you.

THE IMPORTANCE OF BEING A GLOBAL CITIZEN

When it comes to understanding the world around me, the phrase *global citizen* always comes to my mind. To me, being a global citizen is being someone who understands the world around them and is aware of their impact on it. Global citizens take pride in making their community better and becoming involved in organizations, programs, and everyday tasks that make the world a better place.

We are all small elements that make up a larger picture. Everything we do, how we interact with the world, and how we view the world play a large role in our environment and the international community. By being open to learning about those around you, embracing differences, and creating a space where you seek to understand, you are on track to becoming a global citizen.

How we engage with the world is so important. It's key to understanding how interconnected our globe is. Staying involved and being aware of the issues going on in other places allows you to be mindful of what different people, places, and communities are enduring.

Creating a better tomorrow has always been a daily goal of mine. I always ask myself, *What am I doing today that will create a better world for us tomorrow?* I continue my education, I push myself out of my comfort zone to learn new languages, I volunteer in my community in all the places I live, and I treat those around me with kindness and love. Going out of your way to give back to the world and pushing yourself out of your comfort zone can fill you with so much happiness and is very rewarding. Knowing that I can offer a helping hand or guidance to someone who needs it always make my day.

There's no rule that says you must travel to be a global citizen. No matter where you are, you can always open your heart and find ways to understand those around you. No matter where you are, you can always offer a helping hand, a kind gesture, or a moment to listen. No matter where you are, you have the power to create a better tomorrow. Take it upon yourself to understand the issues happening in your community as well as the international community. Find ways to get involved with social causes you care about and be part of positive change for the future.

I have fallen in love with understanding and helping those around me and being part of positive change in both my immediate community and our global community. I hope you take it upon yourself to focus on the issues and people that need it most.

It fills me with the energy to be around those who

are different than me. This may not be the case for everyone, and that's okay. You can find ways to be culturally aware and understanding of differences by watching documentaries, reading books, or even watching a funny film.

Some movies I recommend are

Crazy, Rich Asians, Stuck Together, He Even Has Your Eyes, and *The African Doctor.*

Some family-friendly movies I recommend are

The Karate Kid, Cars 2, Coco, The Sandlot, Kitt Kittredge: An American Girl, Molly: An American Girl on the Homefront, Moana, Mulan, and *The Watsons Go to Birmingham.*

Some books I recommend are

Funny in Farsi, The Culture Map, Bonjour Tristesse, and *The Country Under My Skin (El país bajo mi piel).*

IT'S NOT PERSONAL, I PROMISE

I remember growing up and going through school, not understanding why people did the things they did. The way kids got bullied in school, the way certain people would talk to others, or the way something I wasn't really involved in suddenly became my fault. I would hear the phrases "Don't take it to heart," "They're just going through something," or "They just had a bad day" almost daily. I didn't understand these phrases and always sat there in utter confusion. In third grade, a boy ran up and screamed in my face, "You're so ugly and stupid," and the teacher said, "Oh, don't take it to heart; just ignore him, Sloan." I remember sitting there thinking, *What in the hell do you mean just ignore him?* and *I have no earthly idea what you mean by 'don't take it to heart'*. I was ready to throw my fist directly into this boy's face, and that was the bottom line. Yet every time, and there were many, many times, it always ended up being my fault due to my reaction. Life was filled with situations that I didn't provoke but I somehow became a part of, and I was taking them all to heart. As I got older, I began to ignore the stupid comments, rude boys, and snippy girls and just focus on myself. But even during these times, I didn't understand that absolutely none of it was personal.

It took me until my senior year of college to learn what the concept of projecting was. It took me until then to learn that people were taking things out on me that had nothing to do with me. This was a life-altering realization. The guy yelling at me over a parking spot or the hostess being extremely rude to me had nothing to do with me. I realized that I, too, have taken things out on people that had nothing to do with them. I began to take note of when I did this so I could stop. I also started to notice this dynamic when it occurred in my personal relationships. Every single one of us is trying to navigate life the best way we know how, using the skills we've been taught and acquired through experience. But it's vital that we self-reflect and understand how we impact those around us when we take things out on them inappropriately.

Realizing that people's bad days, insecurities, or anger at the world or their lives has nothing to do with me filled me with a tremendous amount of peace. People's decisions or words can heavily impact and hurt you, which is why it's important to choose the people you surround yourself with wisely. If you have relationships in which you recognize this dynamic at play and want to continue these relationships in a successful and healthy manner, a large amount of communication and healing is needed. People's lack of self-growth or healing can cause them to intentionally or unintentionally hurt those around them, which can cause major issues in friendships and relationships.

When you realize this behavior isn't personal and most likely has to do with the other person's internal struggles, you can distance yourself if needed. Now that I have this perspective, I'm far kinder to people who behave this way. I know that deep down, they're struggling with situations of which I'm not aware. I choose not to let it affect me, and I try never to take it to heart. I can now better handle emotionally tough situations because I know in my heart it has nothing to do with me. I'm not always successful in this, but I'm always aware and am able to help myself remain at peace through it. I focus on my personal growth and healing and make my well-being my priority, regardless of what is being thrown my way.

Find time to reflect on how you handle your bad days or life situations. Consider what steps you could take to stop taking things personally and increase your inner peace. The clarity and comfort I have received since I have gained this mindset are amazing.

So the next time someone's bad day gets projected onto you, remind yourself that it's simply not *personal*.

THE LOVE I HAVE FOR OTHERS

In a world that is ever-changing and filled with both the good and bad, I find myself wanting to hold grudges at times. I want to be mad at those who have hurt me, not taken me seriously, or have damaged my life. Usually, the anger eventually vanishes, but I try to grab it back. I want to be angry at these people, but I can't. I always end up sad and many times in tears. At the end of the day, I know they have things going in their lives that they struggle with, or their past struggles have tainted their view on the world, relationships, friendships, and other situations. I know I don't understand all the struggles that different people go through, but I do know that regardless of the hurt I've felt, I'll always have love for others. I'll continue to wear my heart on my sleeve, find forgiveness for those who have wronged me, find forgiveness for the unthinkable situations life throws at me, and find love in every situation.

As human beings, in some ways we change like the weather, but our core elements usually don't change unless we actively work at it. This can be both comforting and alarming. Sometimes people exit our lives because their paths don't align with ours, but then they return to our lives after they've worked on themselves and blossomed. Some people will return to our lives with their core elements unchanged, showing that regardless of the timing, we'll never align.

I love the way people interact. One of my favorite things to do is sit in a coffee shop to do my work. Coffee shops are filled with friendships, success, vent sessions, tears, exuberant smiles, intelligence, creativity, and a sense of belonging. I don't think I've ever been in a coffee shop where I haven't felt at peace or a sense of belonging. How interesting is that? It's the people who surround us, the strangers we don't even know, who create the beauty of these spaces, and for that, I'm forever grateful.

It's the way I walk down the streets of Barcelona, London, Chicago, New York City, and Antigua surrounded by absolute strangers but feel so connected and comfortable. The love I have for others is strong. I'm even thankful for the strangers I've never met or who have never spoken to me, because they've helped all create the wonderful spaces I have journeyed through on my adventures across the globe.

I love the intense beauty in smiles, laughter, and the comfort in knowing kindness is a language that we all understand. It's the feeling I have when I get off the plane and see families reuniting, filled with happiness and excitement. Couples fall into each other's arms, embracing with tenderness. This is why I have love for others. For all the experiences and feelings they give me, which they will never know.

It's the way I get nervous for the first day of school but find comfort in knowing that everyone else does too, no matter my age or where I am in the world. It's the way strangers start conversations with me about my shirt that says Chicago or that I remind them of their daughter. It's the way we're all interconnected with those around us.

People we don't even know leave impressions on us that we don't even realize. They, too, become a part of our stories, our healing, our growth, and our lives.

The intricacy of humanity never fails to amaze me. The way you can relate to a stranger over a relationship issue, the dislike of the same food, or being from the same area. It's beautiful. It's the reason I'll always wear my heart on my sleeve and forever give love and kindness to those around me. Especially the strangers who are pieces of my experiences in coffee shops, plane rides, train rides, library sessions, and fast-food stops—you are the reason I have love for others.

It's the kindness and love that you can give freely that are your superpowers. You're impactful even when you don't feel like you are. You are memorable, and your love is everlasting. So even if we change like the seasons and find ourselves shedding our skin to begin again, remember we are all a part of someone's story. We are impacting people we might not even remember. So move with kindness and empathy, and fill society with authentic love.

Humanity is effortlessly unique. It brings me joy to be a part of it, and I hope that no matter how high or low the roller coaster of life takes you, you always take time to reflect and give thanks for the exquisitely mesmerizing world around us.

CHAPTER 3

The Complexity of Humans

I remember taking psychology classes during my undergraduate career and thinking that humans were so deeply complex. I was fascinated by the different ways the brain worked. How people reacted in certain situations, how different factors played such a large role in who a person is, and how some topics could be so sensitive based on an individual's feelings, experiences, trauma, or life events. I remember being younger and reacting so harshly to situations. I would take my anger or sadness out on just about anyone around me. As I got older, I realized how inappropriate that was, and how much I hated it when people did it to me. Just because we have a bad day or bad things happen to us does not mean we have the right to take it out on other people. This is why understanding your emotions, your reactions, and your triggers is so important.

We are complex beings traveling around on this floating rock—let's do our best to be kind, compassionate, and learn about ourselves while we're here. I recently took an intercultural effectiveness quiz, and the results were astonishing. The director of my training gave some insight into our results, and she explained that our scores were a reflection of who we were exactly at the moment we took the exam. I found this extremely enlightening. The area where I scored the lowest was self-awareness. I was shocked by this because I thought I was very self-aware. Then I began to think about what my director had said about the results being about who we were right in that very moment. I'm in graduate school, typing articles daily, writing this book every day, and I spend little to no time reflecting on myself. This was a very important realization for me because it enabled me to adjust and make time in my days to reflect on my strengths and weaknesses. I was able to start being conscious of my effect on the world and those within it. We may think we are self-aware and that we fully understand how we affect others, but the truth is most of us aren't. By taking steps such as self-assessment quizzes, journaling, mindfulness, and reflection time, we can create a space to actively work on our self-awareness.

Even though people are complex, there's beauty in complexity. The world is filled with different situations, types of people, and ever-evolving society. In this chapter I touch on the topics of empathy, holding on to people who feel like sunshine, and how showing compassion can help stop some pretty horrific things from occurring.

EMPATHY

Having empathy is key to understanding individuals in our society. Empathy is how aware, understanding, and sensitive we are to the experiences of others. It's a very important aspect of friendships and relationships, yet also imperative in situations with strangers. Being able to pick up on the emotions of the people around us allows us to react accordingly.

Empathy aids us in interpreting others. Understanding other people's perspectives, emotions, intentions, and experiences is crucial when it comes to creating and maintaining healthy relationships. Exercising empathy can also dramatically increase the quality of all our relationships.

THE IMPORTANCE OF EMPATHY

There's great value in trying to understand those around us. Actively working to place yourself in the shoes of others will help you understand both who they are and their position in life.

Increasing the number of empathetic people in our world starts with teaching this skill to children. Teaching children empathy can be done in many ways. For instance, we can talk to children about understanding feelings— both their feelings and our feelings. As parents, siblings, family members, or babysitters, we can model empathy by showing it when a child has a strong emotion, such as fear or anger. Children's feelings should always be acknowledged because they are important, and it's critical they're aware of this.

We can model empathy in conversations with children after certain situations. For example, if you were to ask a child, "How do you think your sister felt when you pushed her to the ground?" this would encourage the child to think about and understand her sister's perspective. This should be done as a calm discussion during which the child can feel comfortable vocalizing her thoughts on the situation and how her sister might have felt.

Even with adults, it's still possible to teach empathy. Usually, adults are taught empathy through training or courses. They can be provided by an employer, required by an employer, or simply done for personal reasons. These courses are filled with models of how respond empathetically in life situations.

However, you don't need to pay for or attend empathy training to become more empathetic. We can teach ourselves and work on increasing our ability to empathize simply by being more mindful of the emotions, expressions, and verbal cues from the people around us. Once you become accustomed to making an effort to understand these elements, you can go a bit further and allow yourself to feel other people's emotions and place yourself in their shoes.

DEAR EMPATHS

Now that you know what empathy is, how important it is, and how to increase it, let's talk about how to navigate the world as an empath. I'm extremely empathetic, and although that may be an amazing thing for those around me, it has also taken a toll on me at times.

Setting emotional boundaries is crucial. It's not your job to carry other people's emotional baggage. It's extremely draining—I'm sure you've experienced this to some extent.

Being able to say no is important. The more weight you carry from others, the less you able you are to attend to your own needs. Empathy is a strength, but I've been in positions where it felt like a weakness. I have felt things so deeply and understood others so well that it ended up really hurting me.

That's when I began to realize the power of setting boundaries. I could set boundaries that allowed me to care both myself and others. Don't feel bad for saying no to your friends when they ask you for a million different favors. It's a compliment that they're asking you. They know you will help, and they know how much you care. However, they may also know that you will feel too bad to say no, and that's a problem. I think sometimes we fear that our friends or family will be upset with us when we set boundaries or say no to something that we don't want to do. This does happen at times, but it's important to remember that it's not your fault. People take out things on us that have nothing to do with us and are out of our control. Again, it's not your job to carry the weight of people's problems.

If you're an empath, I'm sure you often feel overwhelmed with emotions. I'm sure you have been told that you feel too deeply or are simply too emotional. Please understand that you have a high emotional intelligence, and this is your strength. It's important we spend our time with people who don't shame us for this strength or say unkind things about it. The people you choose to have in your life should be picking you up when you're down and making you feel loved and appreciated, not abusing your exceptional ability to empathize.

YOU ARE MY SUNSHINE

Do you know those people who radiate love, light, and support? The people who raise you up and make the bad days good and the good days great? Those people are my sunshine. They fill me with encouragement and shower me in love.

They don't drain me. They don't stand in my light.

They let me be exactly who I am.

It's vital that we find people in life who embrace us and love us for who we are. None of us are perfect, but we're all so beautifully unique.

It took me a while to realize that my circle of people shouldn't drain me; they should do the opposite. They should empower me, love me, and allow me space to grow, feel, and learn. They should leave me feeling refreshed, inspired, loved, and cared for.

I'm thankful for the people who shower me with light and love. I'm falling in love every day with the life I'm creating, who I'm becoming, and the people I surround myself with.

To my friends and family - thank you for being my sunshine. Thank you for being you, and I will always be here to shower you with love, light, and happiness back.

You deserve all the love this world has to offer. You deserve to be surrounded by sunshine.

MAKING THE WORLD A BETTER PLACE, EVEN IN THE SMALLEST WAYS

I'm currently sitting and reading a book for my terrorism class. As I read through the complexities of terrorism and the ways it changes our world, I begin to fall deep into thought. The words of the book are no longer being read to simply study for the exam; they begin to hold a much deeper meaning, as many things in life should.

I'm thankful for my ability to love others, understand others, and empower those around me. I'm thankful for the world we live in, even at its most unbearable times. When the world is in turmoil or destroys people and places that should have never been hurt, I feel a deep ache in my heart. But what others don't understand is that destruction, death, and violence bring communities closer together. I was extremely young on 9/11, and I don't remember the moment it happened. What I do remember is the tears on that date every year as we stood together and said the pledge of allegiance. With my hand over my heart, my teachers and classmates crying around me, and the videos of the destruction bringing me tears even at age five, I learned the power of community very quickly. I remember the moments so vividly, the children in my class whose parents, relatives, or friends had passed that day. I remember the intense BBC news on the radio in the car every morning on the way to elementary school. I remember in sixth grade when we cried tears of joy, strength, and community because Osama Bin Laden had been killed. My teacher expressed how important this was for our country, and although I felt the relief and joy of this accomplishment, I couldn't understand how a person or group of people could have done this to my home. All that time, I had thought it was some sort of bad accident, but my eyes were opened that day. I remember going to New York City with my mom, looking up at her, and asking why it happened because I simply could not wrap my head around it. Even now, at twenty-two years old, it's still very hard. She told me that many people were still hurting, and it wasn't acceptable to talk about it in public. That was something that little me also didn't understand. My curiosity for international relations sparked quite young after being so invested in what President Bush was doing overseas and at home as I listened every morning from my booster seat on the way to elementary school. It hurts me to think that some people come to a place in their life where they feel they have no other options or the only way they know to identify is through violence or support of violent actions. This is not a lesson on terrorism; it's a lesson on perspective and gratitude. It's the idea that the complexity of the world affects each one of us. If I had grown up in a different country, I'm positive I would have other events and memories engrained in my mind that shifted my ideas on the world and created the lens I saw through; no one is excused from the harsh realities that the world brings us. Reading about victims that span the globe makes me feel that although I may not be able to single-handedly fix terrorism, violent extremists, or people with hurtful intentions and capabilities, I can spread infectious love and kindness. I hope that people never feel as if they don't belong in this society and that they, too, see the world in a brighter light. I can't fix everything—no one can. I'm aware that giving love and kindness to others can't undo years of corrupt or immoral thinking, but it can help make our world a better place and may broaden the perspectives of many people I encounter.

I'm thankful for the experiences I've had throughout my life, and I'm thankful for every person I've met, regardless of the type of impact they had. I'm thankful for my ability to make my own decisions, smile at strangers, be understanding, and be empathetic. I hope to make the world a better place by bringing exponential amounts of love and gratitude into the world. I want people to always feel like they are enough, and I strive so deeply to understand the world around me.

For much of my college career, I felt as if I was just going through the motions and wasn't really learning. Yet here I am, almost five years into it, and I realize the profound effect it has had on my perspective. The way I see other people's positions is based on the situation they are in or what they've had to endure. It makes me understand why they think, feel, vote, act, and see things a certain way. This class in particular has provided me with many ways to view, understand, and define terrorism, and that allows me to realize that we are all just people. It was scary to realize that, in essence, anyone could become a terrorist or carry through with violent actions, but it's comforting to know that spreading kindness, love, the acceptance of different religions, people, and ways of life can be enough to stop at least one person from falling into the black hole of terrorism. This idea can be applied to many different aspects of life.

When you see someone eating alone, being outcast or bullied, be the person who asks if they are okay. Be the person who lets them know they are not alone. Be the person who stands up for what is right. Teaching children the importance of loving others is one of the most important lessons they will receive, but not everyone received this lesson or felt loved by others, so even with adults, let them know they are not alone. Offer kindness, peace, and acceptance to those around you.

Life is not easy, and if each of us lend a helping hand, smile at strangers, offer an ear to listen, and share our own perspective, we could prevent people from going to extremes.

I'm thankful for the country I live in; I'm thankful for the countries that have welcomed me with open arms, and I'm thankful for the wonderful different cultures, languages, food, and ways of life that I've been blessed to experience. I hope that by spreading gratitude, empowerment, kindness, and love, we can work together make the world a better place and lessen the amount of hurt that is projected onto people, places, and our Earth. We are a community, every single one of us, and no amount of law, violence, borders, political parties, history, race, culture, or language can change that. It's time we recognize that the issues we face as a society today will take devoted cooperation from every single one of us. If we don't, the dangers we see striking us will continue to hit with increased force. There is no other option but to stand together.

HOW MY MINDSET HAS CHANGED OVER TIME

My mindset continues to change as time passes, and for this, I'm very grateful. But I believe that these past two years, due to the pandemic, my perspective on the world has changed quite drastically. It's important to reflect on the ways your perspective has changed so you can be conscious of your growth or lack thereof. I remember when the pandemic hit, I was filled with fear, and when product shortages began, I got very upset at people for buying so many extra things. However, I admit if I had been in those shoes and the supply was available, I may have bought extra as well. As time went on and restrictions such as curfews came out, my inability to hang out with my friends due to fear of the virus filled me with anger and sadness. It's in times like these that we look for something or someone to blame; it helps numb the pain and gives us an outlet. We saw this happen to quite an extent, and still today, we are feeling and going through the horrifying effects that came from placing blame.

I remember racing to get the vaccine and hoping that everyone would run to get it as fast as I did. When this didn't happen, I was confused and concerned. As the pandemic progressed and issues arose, I found myself placing blame on others. I found myself holding anger at those who did not make the choices that I did. However, as time went on, I began to shift the way I thought about the situation. I forced myself to be in the shoes of those with different perspectives, life situations, and circumstances. Doing this allowed me to gain insight into the choices we all make for ourselves. At the end of the day, it's not a matter of who's right and who's wrong. We're all doing our best, making the best decisions we can, and moving through life the best way that we know how. I didn't change my choices, and I will continue to do what I believe is right, but I've learned not to be upset with those who choose differently from me. I've learned not to place blame on those around me and instead focus my energy on understanding them. This is especially helpful in trying times. It helps me have a greater amount of happiness and love for those around me, even if they make different choices. I've also learned to critique my own choices and opinions as harshly as I do others, which has been quite beneficial.

When it comes down to it, we all make the choices we believe are best. I don't think that most people wake up every day thinking about what horrible choices they can make, and even if we view something as a good choice, opinion, or idea, that doesn't mean that other people do.

Finding ways to understand the world around you can be challenging, but it's much easier when you allow yourself the capacity to understand where other people are coming from. Be conscious of when you place blame on other people or things so that you can adjust your thinking. Be mindful of how you spend your energy and thoughts. Opening your mind to other perspectives will give you clarity and peace. It has helped me become a far more accepting person who takes much less to heart.

I hope you take this time to reflect on your own growth and work on being cognizant of the way you react to those who have different perspectives than you. It has nothing to do with changing your mind or the minds of others, but it has everything to do with understanding those around you. In times of uncertainty, conflict, or crisis, it's far more effective to move with love and understanding than it is to move with blame and hate.

Each of us go through different situations, upbringings, struggles, and pain. No matter where we come from, no matter how much money we have, no matter who we know, none of us can escape the harsh realities of life. Finding kindness and love within you to pass on to the world will create a lasting positive impact in ways you didn't even know were possible. So, although humans are complex, making the world a better place for us all doesn't have to be.

CHAPTER 4

Investing in You

This chapter focuses on teaching you how to invest in yourself—doing things for you, by you. Learning how to take time for yourself, create a positive future for yourself, and love yourself is so important. It's not always easy to focus on our own needs and happiness. Life can feel overwhelming, and time can seem to pass in a heartbeat. But learning how to invest in yourself is the key to success. It's the key to a life filled with self-love and fulfillment. In this chapter, I discuss how to be intentional, the art of focusing, time management, decluttering our lives, and financial health. Investing in ourselves is very important, and it does take work. We must listen to ourselves, follow our guts, and become one with ourselves. This chapter offers advice to help create powerful change, choose what empowers and supports you, and find the space to manifest peace in your life.

HOW TO MOVE WITH INTENTION

Being intentional in your life is extremely valuable. It allows you to make a clear, purposeful path. You can focus on what's important to you and act. These actions will be purposeful, goal-oriented, and designed to align you with the path you're meant for.

During our time on Earth, we often find ourselves feeling mixed emotions or having conflicting thoughts or confusion about what choice to make or what direction to take. When this happens, it's important to realize that it is happening. It's vital that you come to terms with these feelings and understand how they can affect your next move.

By doing this, you can evaluate what's important to you and create a purposeful vision. This will provide you with clarity in both your choices and your position. We are given many choices, ideas, and opportunities during our lives. In order to sort through these feelings and major decisions, we must be intentional with our actions.

Some of my intentions are:

- Always treat people with kindness

- Take care of myself no matter the circumstances

- Become the best version of myself so I can one day become the best mom I can be

- Find success in doing what I love

- Stay true to myself

- Find happiness everywhere I go

To accomplish these intentions, I set goals. When things

don't go as planned or people do things I don't expect, I take a step back. I reflect. I understand it's not personal; I feel the emotions I need to, I allow them to pass through me, and I continue to move with intention. My intention is to understand those around me, to see people in a good light, to treat them with kindness, and to never give up on building the best version of myself.

Don't be fearful of your goals, and don't doubt your ability. Create boundaries that allow you to continue working on your dreams and stay on your path. Always remember that the people who surround you become a part of your energy. They become small pieces of your puzzle that you'll look back on when your journey is over.

Once you've decided on your intentional goals and are actively working toward them, keep a strong and determined mindset. Practice gratitude and thankfulness for the lessons that have come your way, the people who have passed through your life, and the situations that have taught you more than any class, book, or mentor ever could.

Some ways to be intentional in your days are:

- Focus your energy on the task at hand. This will increase productivity.

- Be purposeful with your time.

- Appreciate the supportive and important relationships in your life.

Express gratitude. Take time to be thankful for the people in your life by recognizing what it is that they do that's important to you. I'm thankful for my friends and family for many different reasons, but collectively because they love me, care about me, support me, and never question my value.

Take each day as it comes and fill it with intention. May clarity wash over you, and may you fall in love with being intentional. Make the most of your time in this wonderful world and always move with kindness.

MAKE IT HAPPEN

Time management is a timely topic because the pandemic forced most of us to readjust our lives and the way we manage our responsibilities. Now, as we return to some semblance of normalcy with in-person school, jobs, and activities, we have to readjust all over again. Good time management skills have always been important, but never more so than today as we to attempt to adjust to the ever-changing conditions being thrown at us.

UNDERSTANDING TIME MANAGEMENT

Time management is how we plan, organize, and split our time between different tasks. Effective time management is how we accomplish tasks throughout the day in a successful manner and how we make time for the different of obligations we have in our lives.

I want to give insight into my personal experience through the pandemic and education. During the pandemic, professors used large amounts of assignments and an extremely heavy workload to help keep us engaged, learning, and productive during that weird, lonely, and confusing time. In life, it's important to adapt and grow through changes. At times, I felt extremely overwhelmed with the workload, I felt as if it was far too much, and I felt as if I deserved more than three credits for the classes I was taking. However, it didn't matter if I thought it was too much work. It didn't matter how much I complained or moaned and groaned about it. I chose to be a college student during this time, and with that comes a large amount of responsibility. I could have taken a year off, or even two, but I didn't. I'm fully responsible for my choices, the work they create for me, and the ramifications of my decisions.

It's up to you to manage your time and create an effective plan to ensure your work is complete. It's up to you to take the initiative to take control of your schedule and prioritize different elements of your life. It's also up to you to take a realistic look at your situation and correct the issues that need to be addressed. Issues you could be struggling with include mental health, not understanding your schoolwork, working full time while in school, or struggling to meet deadlines at work. Although these issues may not have a quick fix or a complete solution, it's important that we understand how they affect us and our time management. When you're aware of these issues, you can begin to dissect them and find the pathways to effective time management. For example, mental health may always be a struggle, but how can you better the circumstances you're dealing with? Would therapy allow you a place to express your concerns and struggles? Would this give you more time to focus on your happiness and spend less time struggling? Would medication fill the gaps for what therapy can't provide you? Would taking fewer classes per semester while working allow you to spend more time on your schoolwork and feel less stressed at work? You don't need to rush through and struggle to get a degree—just ask a PhD student! Not understanding your schoolwork can be frustrating, and I've felt this many times during my foreign language classes. However, if you can find a tutor or even communicate more often with your professor, you'll find the assignments and subject to be far more manageable. These are the types of questions you need to ask yourself. You'll likely be surprised by the outcome of these personal conversations with yourself. It's up to us to put ourselves in check and address the issues that we face in our lives.

When we find the root of an issue, we can usually work from there to adjust our needs and schedule.

Does the stress of schoolwork cause you to procrastinate? Be honest with yourself. If you said yes, it's okay and very understandable. Let's take another look at the situation. By procrastinating, you're most likely causing yourself more stress than if you simply did your work ahead of time. Schoolwork may not be something you necessarily want to do, but if you're a student, it's your responsibility. You chose this path. You'll perform much better if you acknowledge the importance of your schoolwork and prioritize it. Your effort will likely be rewarded through improved grades, more free time, and best of all, decreased stress.

To me, time management is how I effectively complete my obligations in an efficient manner. This allows me to have more me time. It also allows me to have less built-up stress. It feels good to check assignments, exams, business proposals, grocery shopping, workouts, or meetings off my list.

I advise you to put the obligation you dread the most at the top of your list. Knock it out, get it done, and move on. The more efficient you become, the better quality of life you'll have. One of the major keys to success is efficiency or having high productivity. You'll find that you'll become more mindful of opportunities, and practicing good time management will enable you to take advantage of them. You may now have the time and motivation to take steps to advance in your career, volunteer for a cause, indulge more in your hobbies, or spend more time with your family.

Some ways to create an atmosphere that cultivates high productivity are:

- Complete your tasks in a space with limited distractions. Leave your phone in another area or put it on do not disturb.

- Create daily schedules as a part of your routine. This can be done in the morning or even the night before.

- Block off time to complete specific obligations.

- Make time for breaks. Breaks are essential as they allow us to decompress and foster new ideas.

NEED A NEW HOBBY?

I sometimes find myself complaining about how I have no time to do the things I want or that there's simply nothing interesting to do, which is completely incorrect. I can make time for the things I want to do, and there's always something interesting to do. I've made a list of some new activities I want to try, new hobbies to get into, and maybe I will even spark some new interests!

EXERCISE

- Go for walks with friends or alone (My favorite spots are butterfly gardens or beaches.)

- Go on runs

- Yoga (This can be done at home, in a park, in a studio, or even at the beach.)

- Group workout classes

- Sign up for a gym membership

- Join a club sport (available at university or through your town)

- Self-defense classes

- Go on a bike ride

- Go for a swim

ARTS AND CRAFTS:

- Find DIY things to create for my home (check out Pinterest)

- Have a painting and wine night with friends

- Check out local museums

- Go to a play

- Make pottery

- Go to a paint pottery class

- Gardening

- Make my own soap

- Make my own candle

FOOD:

- Farmer's markets

- Taco Tuesday with friends

- Croissants and wine with friends while watching *Emily in Paris*

- Cooking classes

- Baking night with friends

- Do my own version of the Great British Bake Off

- Have a fondue night

- Do a food from around the world cooking night

- Finding new cafes or restaurants

EDUCATION:

- Start learning a new language

- Find a new podcast to listen to

- Find a new audiobook to listen to

- Start journaling

- Find a new book to read

THE ART OF FOCUSING

As with many things in life, learning the art of focusing takes a determined and conscious effort. It takes a mind that's ready for new experiences and challenges, a mind that's ready to see change. The first step to mental focus is reducing or eliminating distractions around you. You may have children running around all day, be a single parent, pursue school and work, and or be going through a mentally draining time. Whatever it is that you're enduring, whatever your situation may be, you are in the perfect moment to learn the art of focusing. The idea that there's always time to accomplish our goals later only prevents us from doing it. Starting with your situation at hand, the tools you have now, and the person you are now is the best way to invest in your future, your personal goals, and your well-being.

You don't need to eliminate or reduce distractions for a long time to be successful. You can do it in small spurts, and this is usually the most effective way. When distractions are high, and I have many things to accomplish in a day, I usually choose early mornings to create my distraction-free time to work on my mental focus.

This time can be spent reading, writing, working out, cooking, or meditating. Choose whatever you want to focus on. During this time, limit phone time, limit time spent talking to others, and focus solely on the task at hand.

Another way to increase mental focus is through mindfulness and meditation. Mindfulness is when we focus on being present. Being present allows you to rid your brain of distractions and truly be in the moment. Mindfulness helps to create lucidity and will improve your ability to concentrate. Meditation can help reduce the amount of anxiety you have as well as reduce the amount of stress. Lowering your stress and anxiety levels can help you achieve greater mental clarity. Practicing meditation enables you to stay engaged for longer periods of time and increases your attention span, which inevitably increases your ability to focus.

A factor that many people forget is the importance of taking a break. Taking breaks allows us to spend time away from a task and let the mind relax in a healthy way, creating space for new energy and motivation for focus.

Practice makes perfect, so carve out time in your days to focus on the things that you love or want to accomplish. I hope you use this advice as a guiding tool, but never forget that it has always been within you. You are capable and ready to accomplish your goals.

LIFE CLEANSE: THE FULL-LIFE DETOX

You might think of a life cleanse as reorganizing your room and getting rid of junk, but it can also be limiting your time on social media, donating unneeded belongings, and reassessing relationships. Detoxing from different areas in your life is beneficial because it allows you to have a clear space, mind, and life. Over time, many unhealthy habits start to form, stuff piles up, and we forget how little attention we pay to negative things like social media consumption or clutter. Being in the now is the best way to realize that going through a detox is important.

DECLUTTER YOUR SPACE

Reorganizing my space and getting rid of useless things around my home is one of my favorite things to do. Something about moving my couch or putting my desk against a different wall gives me such excitement and makes my space feel new. It's also important to clean and organize your space. Setting time aside to clean and organize can easily become a habit if you stick with it. I find that setting a thirty-minute timer helps me commit to cleaning my space. I notice myself making excuse not to clean, such as being too busy or too tired, but this only creates more work for another day. If you spend thirty or even fifteen minutes a day cleaning your space, you're far less likely to have catch up on cleaning, and you'll be far more at peace in your space. Another way to declutter your space is to donate any old clothes or items you no longer use. This can be hard because you may feel like you need to hold on to certain clothes or items because of their sentimental value, but if you don't use them and they're simply taking up space, let them go.

A FRIEND CLEANSE

Many times, we stay friends with people because they've been in our lives for a while, and we don't really think much about it. Yet, if you were to create a pros and cons list for all the people in your life, would you like the results? The people we spend our time with eventually become pieces of us. Their energy affects us. The way they view the world, speak about others, and speak about themselves also reflects who we are. Think about that, and find time to create your pros and cons list. If you notice someone not treating you well, not bringing you support and positivity, and speaking about others in a disrespectful manner, is that an accurate reflection of you? Once I began to use this understanding to gauge peoples' position in my life, I slowly began to spend less time with people I did not want to be seen as a reflection of.

SOCIAL MEDIA DETOX

Social media can be a great way to kill time or take a break, but the time you spend on it should be limited. Spending too much time on social media can cause insomnia, unhappiness, and false expectations of the world around you. Sometimes, I find myself aimlessly scrolling through pictures I've already seen ten times on Instagram or spending hours watching reels. All versions of social media can take up far too much of our time. Consider setting a timer on your phone so you can be accountable for limiting your screen time.

IT'S OKAY TO CHANGE CAREER PATHS

Wanting to change career paths can be scary, especially if it's a path you been on for quite some time. But just as we change as people, so do our interests and priorities. Life events can alter what's important to you, but so can personal growth and healing. Jumping around aimlessly from job to job may not be the best idea, but on the positive side, it will teach what you don't want to do or didn't like in a job. Staying in a job you don't enjoy or believe in will make you unhappy. At the end of the day, no one has it figured out; we're all going through life trying to find the balance that makes us feel at peace and aligns with who we are. Following are some tools and tricks for changing career paths.

GOING BACK TO SCHOOL

Going back to school is always a great option. Although it's not a necessity when changing career paths, it can be very helpful depending on your field, interests, and level of knowledge in your new career area. However, don't break the bank to get a degree. There are many different scholarships you can apply for, and there are many great online programs available these days. Many companies will pay for you to go back to school and may even allow you to switch positions within the company.

Various degree and certification options include:

- Associate's degree

- Bachelor's degree

- PhD

- Master's degree

- Cosmetology school license

- Teaching English as a Foreign Language (TEFL)

- certification

- Trade school

LEARNING LANGUAGES

As you know by now, I feel very strongly about learning other languages and the skills they can bring to us. Being multilingual can help you widen the range of people you communicate with and understand. Depending on the field you want to focus on, learning another language may help you get there. Some jobs that would need or want you to speak more than one language are:

- International business positions

- English as a foreign language teacher

- Foreign policy research positions

- CIA

- Diplomacy

- International banking and finance

Some great ways to learn different languages are:

- Rosetta Stone

- Duo Lingo

- Au pair

- Immersion school

- TEFL certification

- College courses

FREE CERTIFICATION WEBSITES

There are many free certification websites out there that can help you acquire new knowledge in different areas. I was unaware of this and thought I needed to keep going to school. It was such a relief when I discovered this amazing opportunity.

Some of these sites include:

- Alison

- Google Analytics Academy

- LinkedIn Learning

- Coursera

Many universities, especially if you're already enrolled in one, have certificate options available to you. If you work for a university, there are many ways to get your degree partially or fully paid for as well as take part in different certification programs.

Whatever new path you want to take, know that you can do it. Follow your heart, choose what aligns with your beliefs, and put in the work. Having our interests change, our circumstances change, and our priorities change is just a part of life. Don't let it scare you; let it push you into wonderful new adventures. Life is a continuous journey of growth and change, so embrace the versions of you that are created throughout time. You deserve to be happy and to do what you enjoy.

THE KEYS TO FINANCIAL SUCCESS: THE PATH TO STABILITY

This piece was written with my father, Ed Koester. It holds a very special place in my heart because I have always looked up to his ability to make strategic, smart, and carefully calculated financial decisions. Ed obtained a bachelor's degree in economics from Westminster College in Salt Lake City, Utah and then found himself at Florida State University for three wonderful years of law school. Go noles! Ed is not only an astounding appellate lawyer but also the best dad in the world. Being financially healthy is something that has always been important to him and as I got older, I finally began to realize why.

Financial success may be defined differently for everyone. Some people can take greater risks with less stress about the consequences or can bypass major economic losses. But, for the most part, financial success is defined as a person's ability to live comfortably without putting themselves into a great amount of debt. What is so interesting about debt is its ability to downplay its strengths and oppression. The way it can appear so feasible to get rid of. It almost seems at times that taking out loans is quite beneficial in the long run, when the truth may be much more sinister and crushing. Even if a loan was a good idea in the long run, there was still a major risk with taking on the debt. Especially when you begin to do this in many different areas of your life and at many different times. Put it this way—if you don't have the money now, what makes you think you'll have that money plus more money down the road? No, this is not the time to make up some explanation about the stock market or the current housing market situation. We never know what set of circumstances will come our way and what events will affect the economics of it all—for instance, the pandemic. No one saw this situation coming, and when it did, it affected every single one of us. Our financial capacity became see-through, and our ability to withstand the powerful forces of the pandemic became apparent.

Financial success and stability are intrinsic elements of a great life. Yet, we never really learn about finances in school. We rely on our parents, mentors, friends, or family members to help us learn the rules of finance. But even if we learn how to buy a house, take out a mortgage, or buy a car, we still struggle to learn the ropes of investing and planning for long-term financial stability. Of course, we can read books and educate ourselves on the subject, but I personally learn best when I get to understand the experiences, mistakes, and journeys of other people in conjunction with educating myself on the subject. I like to learn how people went about different financial situations, what went wrong, what went right, and where different choices could have been made.

Having financial stability leads to independence in

many ways and gives you freedom. Freedom to pursue your own choices, whether they are easy or hard choices, allows you the opportunity to make your own decisions when it comes to needs, wants, travel, and any other type of expense. It rids you of restrictions and puts you in charge of your own life.

Investing is the opposite of speculation. Speculation is buying something and hoping that you can sell it for more in the future. Speculation is betting on a trend or the latest, greatest thing for a quick gain. Investing is the slow process of accumulating wealth. Buying a good mutual fund, an index fund, an ETF, or a broad array of marketable securities and bonds over the course of time to create a permanent portfolio is an example of investing. You don't need to read the daily news or wonder about the next federal reserve moves; you need only to form a strong, clear path for the long run. Investing can also mean investing in yourself, either in terms of your health or your job. For example, bettering yourself in college, learning a skill, working on your public speaking, and honing your communication skills are all examples of investing to improve your ability to have a long, healthy, and productive life. Investing is the opposite of consumer spending. Live below your means while saving and investing, and you will have the greatest chance for a secure life. Debt is the amount of money that you owe another. It could be, for example, a student loan, a car loan, or a home loan. Debt is often referred to as the worst sort of poverty. Debt means that you have already spent tomorrow's productivity and paycheck. Debt should be taken on very, very carefully. History is replete with examples of people borrowing money they didn't have the ability to repay, only causing them great pain down the road. Statistics demonstrate that many divorces are directly linked to financial problems associated with debt. When a greater and greater portion of your earning ability is absorbed or taken up by interest and principal payments, it becomes harder and harder for you to obtain financial security, to have funds to invest, and to even buy what you want today because you bought what you wanted yesterday, without having the money. Credit card vacations and high-interest car loans are all certain ways to impair your finances. There are many common myths to be wary of, such as going to the best school you can get into, regardless of the cost, assuming the school will pay for itself. Borrowing a significant amount of money to go to a higher-rank school to obtain a degree that does not lead to immediate productivity can be very oppressive. The money must be repaid regardless of your income. Special programs such as student loan relief programs are complex, require below the normally expected salaries and living, and should only be considered if done solely with a pre-understanding of your ability to qualify when entering into whatever the particular field of study is. The myth of going to the best college you can, studying whatever interests you, and the rest will take care of itself can be very traumatic when carried out. Choosing a school with a good economic balance of cost versus increased productivity and the ability to obtain a job should be at the forefront. A long time ago, Thorstein Veblen wrote a book called *The Theory of the Leisure Class*, where he explained the concept of Keeping Up with the Joneses. Many people go through life wanting to have better than their neighbor, live as well as their friends, and in doing so, buy a house they can't quite afford, a car they can't quite afford, and dinners, movies, clothes, and other expenditures that are just above their means. They put themselves on a perpetual treadmill, where they will never have the opportunity to rest. Although money doesn't buy happiness, living below your means by financial security puts you in a position to handle life's lows and stresses and sleep well at night. Many people tend to exaggerate about their finances, and it can oftentimes seem like everyone around you is doing better, that everyone around you makes more money than you, and that everyone around you has the easy life. In fact, if you look under the hood of all your friend's and acquaintances' finances, you might find a lot of trouble in there, such as high credit card debt, high-interest car loans, mortgages, and so on. I've never met anyone who had wished they had spent more money earlier in their life, but I've met many who have wished they saved earlier in life. It's better to learn wisdom from the experiences of others than it is to find yourself mentally and physically ready for retirement but with no retirement funds upon which to rely. In talking with people in middle age or later and asking what mistakes they feel they made earlier in their lives that are causing them pain and hardship now, the answer usually involves finances and the failure to save. To save and invest. Sometimes people will have speculated when they were younger, trying to invest in the latest and greatest hot thing, buying a house at the top of the real estate market, blindly assuming there was never going be a business cycle again, and essentially putting a noose around their neck of great financial burden. Then, for example, their house fell in value, and they owed more on the mortgage than the house was worth. Other times it's as simple as going to Starbucks a couple of times a day, eating out more often than you can afford to, and essentially not setting aside any money so that any hiccup in life resulted in a bankruptcy or a general crushing financial defeat. The financial problem could have led to divorce or the inability to help a child go to college or achieve an important life dream. The predominant theme being that if you take it for granted that someday in the future you can catch up on the savings you're not making now, or you can compensate for speculative adventures, that tends to not be the case. Those who live below their means and save their money tend to amass financial security and live well with the ability to achieve their dreams. Those who do not end up working with the feeling of tyranny and then ultimately relying on meager Social Security benefits to get in retirement. Such people often must rely on their children for financial assistance as opposed to leaving a legacy to their children. Treating yourself with respect and your finances with respect means taking an objective approach. Entering into a prenuptial agreement to decide, for example, who's responsible for the student loans, should the marriage not work out. It can decide what happens with the respective party's earnings and separate assets such as inheritances and gifts. True love does not have to be incompatible with objected financial truths and self-preservation. At a minimum, prenuptial and postnuptial agreements are taking care of your personal financial health. This makes it possible for the parties to be two tall trees in a marriage, with each having a full understanding of the financial ramifications of life together. Take the time to learn about the basic concepts of a healthy financial life, such as how auto insurance works, how an umbrella policy works, what it means for the way a car is titled, homeowners insurance options, and these types of things. Too many people find out too late that they should've had something they didn't have, that they didn't even know existed, or didn't even realize they did not have. This is especially true of the type of insurance that you ought to have, depending on your circumstances. Becoming fully engaged with these parts of life and learning how they all work will give you both peace of mind and the ability to protect yourself in the long run. Reading about Warren Buffett and his teachings is a great idea to gain an understanding of the differences between investing and speculating. Even reading the Berkshire Hathaway annual shareholder letters can start to give you an appreciation for why not to be concerned regarding market fluctuations. Be an investor, not a speculator or a market timer.

When we invest in ourselves, we create space for the best versions of us. We give ourselves the best shot at a beautiful life. You should always, without a doubt, be investing in yourself. You are your own best friend; you are the person you will always have, every single day. So why would we ever not invest in ourselves? The simple answer is because we make everything but ourselves a priority. Losing yourself to everything around you is longer an option. Make yourself, your dreams, your happiness, and your goals your priority, and always invest in you.

CHAPTER 5

The Power in Letting Go

Before you dive into this chapter, I want you to take a moment to reflect on the progress you've made so far. I'm proud of you for choosing this book, and I'm proud of you for continuing with it. Even if you have struggled to find time to read or take time for yourself, know that you are still making honest and true progress. Many people have not taken the time to actively work on themselves, yet here you are, consciously pushing to be better and making the effort to become the best version of you. For that, I'm extremely proud of you. Never give up.

Do you know the feeling of carrying all the groceries inside in one trip? How good does it feel to set those bags down and relieve your body of all that weight and pressure? It feels amazing. That's how it feels to let go of grudges, hate, anxiety, negative self-talk, and heavy emotions. It makes you feel as light as a feather drifting on the wind. You feel free and capable of anything.

I envision myself dancing in an open field, twirling around in gratitude for myself. The sun shining on my skin and the birds dancing above me. The flowers swaying with the wind and the air so warm and loving. I am, in this moment, free from all hate, negativity, and anxiety.

I feel complete, and I feel loved. I feel loved by myself, and I feel so thankful for my body, mind, and soul. When I envision this feeling, I'm alone in the frame. I alone am enough. I alone capture the entire moment, feeling, and vision. I alone am everything.

Take a few minutes to envision yourself in your most freeing state. Allow your shoulders to drop, your breath to relax, your mind to slow, and release anything weighing down your mind and body.

Now, envision yourself, the freest version of yourself, in your own heaven on Earth.

Take note of what you envisioned. When you feel the weight of the world on your shoulders or the heaviness of not feeling like enough, go back this vision. Remind yourself that this feeling is possible and begin to release the negativity and weight from your body. Let it fall from your fingertips and roll off your shoulders.

We constantly allow things to take us over, and when the weight feels like it's too much, we freeze, and we break down. Let us always remember the power of letting go. The importance of removing toxicity from our lives and creating a positive space for ourselves. It's time we start being so proud of ourselves and so in love with ourselves that we never dare speak to ourselves in a negative manner.

THE POWER OF TAKING A BREAK

Taking breaks is an essential part of life. Breaks allow us to spend time with ourselves and be in the moment. They allow us to recharge and avoid burnout.

Just as little kids fight naps, I used to fight taking breaks. Sometimes, I still do. Yet, I've learned that when I refuse to take a break or ignore my body's cry to take a step back, I suffer. I'm usually far less productive the next day and never fully recharge. This makes my next day's work fall under my desired level of achievement.

This realization helped me see that breaks are profoundly important.

I began to see the impact on my mind and body and the effects of burnout. My experience in graduate school has been filled with imposter syndrome and the constant go, go, go for studying. I will read article after article for hours, research topics for hours, and write and rewrite papers until I believe they're perfect. As the days turn into weeks, I realize the toll it has taken on my body when I don't take time for myself.

Whether you're in graduate school, an undergraduate, or in the workforce, make sure you take time to recharge. You only hurt yourself when you push yourself to unhealthy limits of mental exhaustion.

What I've learned to do is set timers for breaks. It

holds me accountable and reminds me to take a step back. Get some fresh air, eat a meal, and maybe even take a quick nap. Sometimes we're so mentally focused on what's in front of us that we disregard our needs. I believe that when I work far too hard for too many hours, I suffer the next day. That's my body's way of telling me to slow down. It's my body's way of saying, "You know what? You didn't care for yourself, and because of that, you're being forced to take it easy today."

I've had times where I continuously ignored these signals for days, thinking I could overcome the warning signs my body so desperately wanted me to hear. When this happened, I physically felt sick. I felt shaky, uneasy, and had little to no energy. I had no option but to lay down and sleep until my body was ready to rise again.

This is not our bodies punishing us, but our bodies protecting us from burnout. My body wins every single fight, and I've finally, after twenty-two years, given in. I'll listen to its needs; I'll do what it needs me to do make sure I'm safe and healthy.

Here's a list of things I do during my breaks:

- Clean my room

- Take a nap

- Take a shower

- Watch a movie

- Take a bath

- Make a snack

- Take a walk

- Call a friend

Take time in your days, whether it be a five-minute break or an entire evening, to do something for yourself. You are your own built-in best friend; listen to your body and remind yourself that breaks are necessary in order to keep moving.

Sometimes we don't believe that we deserve breaks or that we haven't worked hard enough to be able to take one. This is our negative self-talk interfering. You are always deserving of peace, mindfulness, and a moment away from the world. Learn to be comfortable spending time with yourself and let silence fill you with peace and serenity.

LEARNING HOW TO FALL IN LOVE WITH YOU

Self-love has a different meaning for everyone. In fact, self-love is a multitude of things. What's important is that we learn how to cultivate our own brand of self-love in our everyday lives.

A critical aspect of self-love is growth. Growth creates room for you to enhance your understanding of and appreciation for yourself. Without growth, self-love comes and goes, and that's not fair to you.

We all take care of our bodies differently because we all have different needs—what is key is how you define your self-love.

For me, self-love is listening to my body. This could mean taking an extra day off from the gym because my body is telling me it needs rest. This could mean getting a Starbucks coffee before classes because I am extra excited for my day. This could also mean getting up early, eating healthy, and kicking ass at the gym because I know it makes me feel my best.

Self-love to me is being my own best friend and number-one supporter. Self-love is knowing that no matter what, I'm going to be okay.

It's imperative that we prioritize ourselves and our needs. It's so easy to get caught up caring for others, whether it be a friend, coworker, or significant other, but we must always come back to ourselves and our needs. Take time out of the day to focus on you. This can take the form of reading, taking a walk, meditating, practicing yoga, taking a hot bath—whatever makes you happy. I think we fear that taking these blocks of time for ourselves will decrease our effectiveness, or we're convinced we're so busy that we don't have time. Why is our personal time the first to be tossed during a busy day? Because we choose to prioritize other things.

Learning how to trust yourself will give you so much freedom. You are capable of amazing things, and you need to tell yourself that until you wholeheartedly believe it. No matter what stage of life you're in, I'm sure you feel some sort of stress about the future. This can create anxiety and can lead you to question your choices and decisions. Trusting yourself will help decrease the amount of anxiety you feel when facing tough decisions about the future.

Some ways to cultivate trust in yourself include:

- Write down your goals and how you will accomplish them. What steps do you need to take to fulfill these goals?

- Step out of your comfort zone. Your mind and body are incredible; push yourself. It will make you proud of what you can accomplish.

- Manifest. Take time to visualize your most successful, happy, and healthy self. What do you look like? What are you doing? Visualizing is simply not enough. You must want to feel the change. Start showing up as this person. Start making the necessary changes to get to this envisioned self. You can do it.

When we finally release the weight that has been sitting on our shoulders, we feel free. We begin to blossom, and we begin to find ourselves. Letting go helps us make new beginnings and embark on new journeys. If you don't let go of the weight you're carrying, you'll stay stuck in the same spot, struggling to make progress. I hope you're able to find the strength to let go and be free from all things that are holding you back, consuming your life, and keeping you from being the best version of yourself.

Letting go of things is not always easy, whether it be people, experiences, or memorable items. It's okay to take a break during this time and let yourself feel the pain, sadness, or hurt. Every time you take a break, you make space for something new. Every time you're hurt and comfort yourself, you practice being your own best friend and biggest supporter. You begin to internalize the knowledge that you're strong, capable, and loved.

I'm rooting for you to find the strength to change your life for the better in every way possible. I'm here to give you guidance the best way I know how, which is through my writing. I'm here to show you that even though I may not know you, I know you're strong enough and capable of creating the life you want, no matter what your stage of life.

This life is a beautiful journey, and I'm thankful you're

here to experience it. I'm excited for your progress and the changes that you'll make.

SOME THINGS DON'T NEED FIXING

It's always interesting when we find ourselves making excuses for someone else's words or actions. Whether it be a partner, friend, neighbor, or coworker, when people treat you like shit, it's not your job to justify it or switch the narrative so that the outside world doesn't view it as bad.

I understand having a bad day or making a mistake, but don't get it twisted. We should not be making the same mistake over and over in different forms, and we should not have a bad day for most of our days because that is a pattern of behavior. It's a pattern that no one wants to be woven onto their quilt of life, that's for sure.

Often there's nothing we can do in these situations. These people need to go to therapy, find self-love, partake in healing, or resolve past traumas, which is fine but needs to be consciously recognized. It needs to be recognized because we should not be taking the brunt of someone's past trauma or unresolved issues. We should not be mental punching bags for other people.

Recognizing this toxic behavior starts by seeing situations for what they are and not what you want them to be. It starts by being honest with yourself and trusting yourself enough to walk away from mentally draining, unhealthy relationships. At times it may feel like you've reached a dead end with people. Nothing is getting better; nothing is changing, yet you stay. You stay because you feel like there's hope or a chance it will become better. Sometimes, it does get better. With dedicated effort, communication, and a mutual effort to solve unhealthy patterns, it can get better.

I'm not a relationship expert, but I know which feelings I don't enjoy having. I know which behaviors I don't enjoy being around or that don't make life better. I don't enjoy having someone's bad day projected onto me because they wanted to take it out on someone. I don't enjoy feeling bad about my accomplishments because someone wanted me to feel insecure to make themselves feel better. I don't enjoy expressing my feelings and getting gaslighted. I don't enjoy getting mixed signals because of another person's instability. I notice that when I allow these situations to happen, they repeat, and they repeat until I refuse to tolerate it anymore and move on. This is what I mean when I say, "Some things don't need fixing." I'm not on a mission to fix everyone around me. I'm living my life to the best of my ability, and I want to become the best version of myself I can be. If I let others fill me with this type of energy, it only makes sense that it would have a negative effect on me.

Sometimes we can be the ones projecting our issues onto others. No one is perfect; these things can happen to us all. However, if we're the problem, it's important that we acknowledge it and refocus on our healing. It's unacceptable to purposely hurt others on our healing journey. It's unacceptable to use people around us to fill the gaps within us. Don't drag other people into your personal journey and certainly don't take it out on them.

I personally believe that life is too short to play a constant tug of war with people. It's too short to deal with shit every day. It's too short to have more bad days than good. What I've learned is if we cut it off kindly and move on, we free ourselves and open the door to self-healing and self-love. I used to think it was an inevitable part of life, dealing with all these issues, and sometimes it is, but the difference is now I get to choose. I get to choose my friends, my partner, and what I allow in life. I get to choose how I react to these situations; I get to choose how I overcome these situations; and I get to choose when to walk away from these situations. It all comes down to taking back your power and understanding your worth.

I'm consciously working daily to remove toxicity from my life and engage with only the healthiest and most genuine energy. I want good days, healthy love, and communication. I want to only allow in what I know I deserve, and for a long time, I downplayed what I deserved. I set the bar very low and put up with whatever came my way. But now, if you don't bring what you should to the table, you can find another place to sit. Life is simply too short to accept anything less than what you deserve. Respect yourself enough to walk away from situations that don't benefit you.

Being alone is not scary. Being alone has given me the gift of learning about myself, traveling the world by myself, writing a book, fulfilling my dreams, understanding my worth, and the freedom to make all my own choices. I've become my own best friend, and I've become a much better person because of my time alone.

So I urge you to stop putting up with the bullshit, stop making excuses for those around you, and simply move on. Just let it be—some things don't need fixing.

HEALTHY ENDINGS ARE IMPORTANT

Good and bad things come to an end many times throughout our wonderful journey here on Earth. People grow at their own rates, their ideas and values change, and they become different versions of themselves at different times during their lives. I used to hold it against people if they were not on the same page as me, but eventually I realized that I wasn't trying to turn to their page and adjust to their situation either. Since we grow at different rates, we can't hold it against someone for not being where we are in life. We experience things differently, we find comfort in different things, we fill our time with what's important to us in that moment, and we have no room to judge others for doing the same. As humans, we make mistakes constantly because no one has the right answer for everything. In a world where we're all so uniquely different, it makes sense that we're all usually on different pages and in different places in our lives.

I find it in myself to understand and support and no longer hold grudges and resentment. Hate is not something I want to fill my mind, body, or soul. I want to be filled with love, light, and support. I want to create a positive and lasting impact on those I meet and spend time with. So if friendships or relationships end in your life and you can create a healthy ending, do it. Take the time to work with yourself to find forgiveness and understanding and continue on your path. By creating healthy endings, we can avoid having angry or hurt feelings residing within us. Instead, we can feel like free birds continuing our journey. To live and to let go, to understand and move on by taking the path of least resistance are the keys to this chapter. Healthy endings are better for all of us, and even if they require uncomfortable conversations and feelings, they lead us to inner peace.

Now that you have a variety of tools to choose from, you can begin to let go of anything holding you back. It's time to put these ideas to the test. Today is the day to start learning to let go in the healthiest way you can. You don't need to clean out the entire house or remove every toxic person from your life at this very moment, but it's time to start being conscious of and actively work toward letting go of the things in your life that are not serving you. Take back your power and learn to let go. I believe in you!

CHAPTER 6

It's Always Been You

As we reach the final chapter of our journey together, I hope you continue to practice self-love, healing, and growth. Life is about continuously learning and our ability to adapt and readjust. It's an incredible opportunity to accomplish your dreams, love the people around you, and enjoy every minute. Life is filled with the good, the bad, and the ugly—it's all about how we perceive them. It's about how we choose to handle these situations. If you need to take a break, that's okay—know that you're strong enough to return and overcome. Know that it's okay to feel heavy emotions and to let difficult times in life soak into you. Let these feelings fill your body and allow yourself the space to feel, reflect, and heal. Envision the flowers intricately closing your wounds, making you whole again, leaving behind freshly made gardens of love and beauty.

SELF-LOVE: GIVE YOURSELF A HUG

As I've already discussed, self-love is a plethora of things. For me, it can mean something different depending on the day, but overall, it means always looking out for myself and holding myself up even on days I don't want to. Some days it means watching movies and relaxing, some days it means running errands and cleaning, and other days it means studying all day. Whatever my mind, body, and soul need that day, I give to it. Self-love is recognizing what we need and giving it to ourselves, listening to ourselves, and making ourselves our priority. Some may argue this should not be the case, but I believe you simply cannot pour from an empty cup. Once the cup becomes empty and it stops getting filled, we begin to reach breaking points, unhappiness, depression, and dissatisfaction with our lives.

I used to fight with myself and push myself to do things I didn't want to or make myself feel bad for taking breaks, time away from the gym, or alone time. Yet, as I've grown older, these things have become extremely important to me. I threw in the towel about two years ago and finally started to listen to my body instead of fight with it.

For example, I used to go to Orangetheory to work out five to six days a week. I was in great shape, gaining weight (which I was proud of), and loving my progress. After about a year, I realized I was becoming unhealthily obsessed with my body image. I was examining how I looked every single day, critiquing it, getting upset with it, no longer appreciating it, and talking down to it.

I decided to take some time off, and that helped me quite a bit, both mentally and physically. I started to appreciate my body for all it does and love my body through all its phases. I've learned to give my body breaks when it needs them and not push it to meet unnecessary standards. During my break from Orangetheory, I found new ways to move my body, such as hot yoga. Now I focus on thanking my body, loving my body, and appreciating what it does for me every day. Different types of exercises and practices are good to explore because sometimes we need change and to focus on the different aspects of our bodies and minds we may have been neglecting.

Taking breaks and rediscovering your balance is very important. They help us reconnect with ourselves and reestablish a relationship with ourselves, our goals, our values, and more.

Another element of self-love that I have a deep appreciation for is alone time. Being alone grants me the space to explore myself, my interests, my values, and who I am as a person. It's important you find who you are and to love yourself through the process. Learning about yourself and understanding who you are in the world will be one of the most fulfilling experiences you have. It's a continuous journey of becoming the best possible version of ourselves. I spend my alone time reading, watching movies, writing articles, grocery shopping, studying, traveling, and working out. Doing activities with yourself is essential because, after all, you are your own best friend. The time you spend with yourself should be your heaven on Earth. You are your own safe haven.

It's also important to spend time with people who value you, raise you up, care for you, and support you. Self-love can be as simple as holding yourself accountable for eating enough even when you're upset or getting up to run errands when you wish you could just hide in bed. Self-love is not accepting the bare minimum and standing up for yourself. Figure out what self-love means to you and live by it.

Simple things I do to show myself love include:

- Making sure I drink enough water

- Get enough rest

- Eat enough

- Read

- Write

- Take baths

- Do my skincare

- Go to the gym

Bigger things I do to show myself love include:

- Follow my dreams

- Follow my heart

- Plan trips and activities outside my comfort zone

- Trust myself and my decisions

- Stand up for what I deserve

- Set boundaries

- Respect myself enough to walk away from toxic situations

GROWING PAINS

Healing is a never-ending cycle, which I'm forever thankful for. It may seem tiring at times, feel out of place or unfair, or cause breaking points, but it's really a beautiful thing. You are constantly forming into the most unique, loving, and confident version of yourself. You are the greatest project you will ever work on. The pains we feel are forcing us to have realizations about not only ourselves but our environment. While this can be scary and uncomfortable, it's also divine.

Life can knock us down and push us into very vulnerable versions of ourselves. This can be felt in the form of instability, indecisiveness, insecurity, and more. What's so beautiful about these feelings is that they give us room to reevaluate and grow.

It's an opportunity to readjust and begin new—another chance given to us to become a better, stronger, more wonderous version of ourselves. Every day is not good, but there is always good in each day. Practicing gratitude during times of pain allows you to see the world in a new light. It reminds you of the magical things that are always there that you may not usually notice. Gratitude allows you to be thankful for your progress, your strength, and your endurance throughout your journey.

So, as you feel yourself breaking down and rebuilding, be thankful for the growing pains. They are a friendly reminder that you are getting closer to the best version of yourself. You are unique. You are beautiful. You are worthy of all the extraordinary things this world has to offer. You are loved. I don't understand why things happen the way they do or why certain things happen to some and not others. The unexplainable happenings of this world will remain a mystery to all of us, but at least we're all in it together.

I hope you embrace the growing pains, every last bit of them. I hope you find it in yourself to be thankful for the process and to find your strength. Use it as a time to find yourself and who you want to be from now on. You can endure anything this world throws at you, and I wholeheartedly believe that. Just as they say it's five o'clock somewhere, there's always someone out there going through their own growing pains at the same time you are. We're all together in this, even if it doesn't seem like it.

UNDERSTANDING THE PUZZLE OF YOU

Learning how to understand ourselves can be an interesting process, but a wonderful one too. It's like a journey of learning that we didn't know we needed. We always hear that school is important, getting good grades is an important aspect of success, and finding a well-paying job is a necessity. But what we don't hear is how important it is to understand ourselves and how important it is that we devote time to learning about ourselves. We might be complicated and confusing beings, but that's because each of us is so unique.

One way I have learned about myself is through writing. I write about what I love, what's important to me, and what I value. This has helped guide me through college major changes, choosing where to attend graduate school, deciding who to stay close to, and what I want to prioritize. It can be as easy as making a list of what you love or what your values are. By doing this, you can see what things steer you from your values or what takes time away from what you love. I hadn't realized how focused I was on what everyone else was doing or how I was forcing myself to excel in things I didn't enjoy because I thought it was the good path to success. I realized how some of the people I was spending my time with did not have the same types of values as me. It showed me how important it is to find people who align with what is important to me. One of my values is empathy because it gives us the ability to feel and understand those around us. It allows us to open our hearts and care about other people, whether it be a stranger or a best friend. I value this so strongly because I know how important empathy is in this world, especially with the hard times we all find ourselves in at one point or another. I realized some people didn't care to understand those around them, and they focus solely on themselves. This negatively affected me because I feel so strongly about understanding and giving love to those around me.

By writing down your values, what you love, and what's important to you, you can learn to better under-stand yourself. It's okay for the things we love, prioritize, and value to change, which is another great reason to write these important puzzle pieces down. Another way I learn about myself is through my time spent alone. I used to feel like I always had to be with other people or constantly be doing things, but as I got older, I realized how inaccurate this is. I learned how wonderful it is to spend time with myself, to learn about my strengths and weaknesses, to find the path I was meant to be on.

It's my hope that you fall in love with learning about yourself and that you create time and space to spend with yourself. You are important, you are cared about, and I know you will fall deeply in love with yourself as soon as you start to understand the puzzle of you.

NO ONE KNOWS YOU LIKE YOU DO

We constantly hear people saying things about us; whether it be good or bad, someone is always talking. It does keep things interesting, I admit. I'm always finding things out about myself from others that I didn't know before (kidding!). It's important to remember that no one knows you like you do. You don't need other people's opinions, help, or ideas to direct your life. You should listen to yourself in times of doubt, excitement, and decision-making. People give unsolicited advice all the time. They'll tell you what you should do, what you're good at, where you should live, and who you should be with. Even if they've known you for years, they don't know you better than you know yourself.

You are in charge of yourself and your life. You are

the leader of your decisions. Your best friends, family, and those closest to you can help support the decisions you make, but they should not be influencing you to do something because they want it for you, or they just feel that it's best for you. They could love you more than anything in the world, but they don't know every detail of your life, emotions, goals, and wants. You may still be figuring these things out as well, which is why you should listen to yourself above all. Listen to your gut and follow your heart. It has never been about the destination—it's about the journey. If we focus too hard on the destination, we lose sight of the beauty of the process. We forget that we're passing through time that we'll never get back. The adventure life takes you on when you follow your heart and fall in love with finding different dimensions of who you are is far more important than the destination, wherever it may be.

You are not what people say about you, and you are not how people treat you. You are who you are. You are how you decide to treat people. You know yourself. You know your abilities. You get to decide who you are and who you are not, not the people around you. So amid the unsolicited advice, the twisted situations, and inaccurate descriptions of you, may you never forget that no one knows you like you do.

WHAT YOU FIND WHEN YOU LOOK WITHIN

Looking within can be a choice, but it's not always a choice. Many times, we can find ourselves facing issues and dealing with great amounts of pain and confusion. It's interesting how we can see the issues in other people's relationships, friendships, toxic patterns, but it's so hard for us to recognize our own. Until we're faced with a situation and receive similar results, can we find ourselves truly looking within. I've had uncomfortable realizations about my own patterns, toxic traits, and insecurities. It's not fun for anyone to realize negative things about themselves, and it can be a hard pill to swallow. But when we look within, we find pieces of ourselves that we have never noticed before. Little pockets of hurt and suffering we may have ignored for years. We see broken boundaries, areas where we have been walked on, cries for help that we have muffled over time, and wounds that we pretend not to have. What we see when we look within is a work in progress. But it's a beautiful work in progress that deserves our love, guidance, and attention.

This year, I have focused much of my energy working on my inner growth. I've worked on discovering the patterns that I tend to follow, the behaviors I tend to allow, and how I react in certain situations. I've worked on realizing them in the moment instead of after the fact. I've worked on not resenting those who don't align with me, and I've learned to love and simply be free.

What I've especially learned is that we can choose to look within and be proactive with our growth, or we can wait for life to force it on us. Both choices are not fun, but one choice leaves you in a far better position to start on the path to bettering yourself.

One thing I've struggled with is believing that living in another place would be better or different. If I'd chosen a different school, I would have made more friends, had more fun, or gotten a better degree. If I'd gone to undergraduate in London, my life would be spectacular now. But no matter how far I wander, there's no escaping what's within. No one can heal your wounds but you. No one can choose happiness for you. Sometimes life seems like a never-ending game of strategy and confusion. But when it does stop, we can no longer play the game of life. We can no longer create new goals and change ourselves, our actions, or our effect on the world.

Other places may have different cultures, languages, food, and people, but what's inside you stays the same. What drove you to seek something better or different is still there; just the scenery is different. This is not something to fear, just something to be aware of. Be conscious of the way you handle situations, talk to yourself, and handle pain or trauma. It's not vulnerable to look within and understand these things about yourself. It enables you to create healthier relationships and give love to others.

I still have much growth to do as a person, as we all do, but I fall in love with life every single day now. When I face challenges, I'm thankful that I'm here to navigate them. When things go wrong, I take it as a lesson to learn from. I wish nothing but the best for those who are no longer in my life, and I have nothing but love for anyone who has ever been part of my wonderful journey. They're all pieces of my life puzzle—a representation of experiences, love, lessons, learning, understanding, and gratitude.

I want to leave a positive impact on those I encounter, and I hope that when they think of me, they think of how capable they are and how loved they are.

I want everyone in this world, especially you, to know deeply loved you are. Don't be hesitant to look within. You're strong enough to put the pieces back together in the healthiest shape possible. You're everything you ever needed, and I hope you never forget that.

THE SPACE YOU TAKE UP AND ITS SIGNIFICANCE

You are important. You deserve to take up space. You should feel proud of the space you take up. You should never feel bad about taking up space. You should never feel like a burden for taking up space. And with that, I will begin.

When I was younger and far more unsure of myself, I didn't want to take up space. I didn't want to call attention to myself. I wanted to blend in. Even though I have come far from this mindset, I still find myself wondering if I'm taking up too much space or if I need to be less. When I feel like this, it's because I feel bad for being all that I am, though I have no reason to be. There's no reason why anyone should feel bad about being everything they are. The accomplishments we achieve, the goals we reach, the life we create for ourselves should always take up space, and that should never be downplayed. The space you take up is important, and it sets the tone for who you are and what you will tolerate. The second you feel even slightly bad for your accomplishments, goals, or dreams, you need to have a talk with yourself. You deserve all the space you take up, and you should never diminish the importance of that—ever.

We are all amazing beings who hold different talents, unique abilities, love languages, personalities, and goals. Different things in life are important to each of us. We hold the space we take up by being proud of these differences and not allowing anyone to dim our light. When I let people downgrade what I had done or accomplished, I let them shrink the space I took up, which made me feel as if

I were less. I should have stuck up for myself and held my space. Today, if someone tries to downplay my ability or accomplishments, I respectfully tell them to *fuck off*. I take up my space, and I continue. I'm no longer worried about being too much or taking up too much space. Taking up space has shown me to stand up for myself, take less shit from others, and continue working on my goals.

I hope you find it in yourself to own your space and not allow anyone to downplay your abilities, accomplishments, or dreams. Never feel as if you need to be less to accommodate someone else. Let them go find that somewhere else. Life is not a costume party where we dress up to play the part. We are who we are, and we need to be ourselves unapologetically.

IT'S THE LITTLE THINGS IN LIFE

Being happy or finding happiness may appear as some arduous task, where everything must be perfect in order to obtain it. But this could not be further from the truth. In all honesty, I've found happiness in the smallest moments every single day. It's about how we view happiness and what it means to us. For me, happiness is being at peace, being thankful, and enjoying the process of life. I don't need the perfect job or to have it all figured out to be happy. Thank goodness, because that would be difficult, to say the least. Part of my happiness comes from the freedom I have to choose my path and make my own decisions. Part of my happiness comes from the support system around me. My happiness comes from many different things, which is what I believe creates a happy life. You don't have to be dependent on your pay raise or your significant other to be your main source of happiness. You can be full of happiness because of who you are and what you choose to view as happy and fulfilling. Some little things that give me happiness are fresh cups of coffee, seeing my friends smile, blooming flowers, receiving my food at a restaurant, watching my friends succeed, ladybugs, butterflies, sunny days, rainy mornings, and good music. The little things make such a positive impact in my life, and they are how I find happiness in many of my days.

Happiness is also a mindset—a way of navigating life. We can choose to focus on the bad, feel empty because of one missing piece, or refuse to see the good, which will negatively impact us. The world is filled with pieces to fill you and make you feel full again. When emptiness strikes or negativity clouds your mind, remember to take a step back. Start fresh, and let the world fill you with the little pieces of happiness it has to offer daily. Taking a walk on the beach, feeling the sand beneath your feet, watching the waves effortlessly crash, hearing the birds chirping, and seeing the crabs busy at work are all ways to let the world fill you with happiness. If you don't feel strong enough to find it yourself or don't know where to look, just step outside. Allow the fresh air to fill you and recharge you. Let it guide you. Let it teach you that there's happiness everywhere, no matter how far you wander. It's all about our perspective and what we will allow in, what we allow to become a piece of us. I will always let in the happiness the world has to offer, and I will search for the good in every place that I am because I want to be filled with the most beautiful parts of life. The Earth will always provide us with pieces of happiness to absorb if we just find the time to look for them and open our minds to accept these wonderful gifts. Finding happiness in the little things will let you regenerate your happiness, creating a never-ending cycle of being filled. Sometimes we look for our happiness in people, jobs, accomplishments, or money, but doing this makes it far harder to fill yourself back up when that person, position, or money leaves. When you gain happiness through a multitude of areas, such as through hobbies, exercise, writing, or cooking, each piece comes together to fill you up. If you lose one of those pieces, the gap to fill isn't that large. Just like multiple streams of income can be beneficial, so can multiple streams of happiness.

GIVE YOURSELF THE CREDIT YOU DESERVE

No matter how big or small the accomplishment, you should always give yourself the credit you deserve. I am beyond proud of you for coming on this journey with me. You're still here, finding ways to love yourself, better yourself, and to stop putting up with shit, and because of that, I sit here smiling from ear to ear. I don't need to know you to know how capable and beautifully unique you are. I don't need to know you to tell you that you're more than enough and that you're amazing. The impact you make on the world by just being in it is indescribable. There's no one else like you. You're the only version of you on this entire planet. No one can be you, even if they try their hardest. No one can recreate your uniqueness, quirks, the way you smile, the way your hair falls, the way you view the world. These are all unique to you. It's time to own your worth. It's time to understand your power, potential, and breathtaking ability.

I don't want you to try to force yourself to be like anyone else. I don't want you to try to make yourself like things you never will. I want you to be you. I want you to stay true to yourself because I wouldn't want this world to miss out on such a wonderful person.

So give yourself the credit you deserve. On the hard

days, give yourself a hug and thank yourself. Thank yourself for the wholehearted strength of your body and mind. On the good days, embrace it and live fully in the light. Enjoy your moments in their entirety and stay away from anyone who does not allow you to have this experience. Giving yourself credit on the bad days is just as important as giving yourself credit on the good days. It's about self-love, self-acceptable, and the ability to be proud of yourself. You should be happy for yourself and excited about everything you thrive in, regardless of how big or small.

Never sell yourself short, and make it a priority to celebrate every single win, even if the win is simply making it through another day. Every win counts, and you deserve to celebrate every step along the way. Find happiness in the little things. Take time to fall in love with yourself and spend time with yourself. You are important. You are strong. You are needed here on this Earth. And although this may be the end of our journey together, it is just the beginning of yours. May this adventure of self-exploration and healing bring you love, light, freedom, happiness, and everlasting support. I'm always rooting for you. It has always been you.

P.S. This book loves you.

ABOUT THE AUTHOR

SLOAN is currently an international affairs master's student at Florida State University. She obtained a bachelor's degree in International Studies and minored in French at Coastal Carolina University in 2021. With a passion for international affairs and languages, she has spent many years studying French and, in December 2021, spent a month in Guatemala at a Spanish immersion school in Antigua. She is passionate about traveling, creating healthy and inspiring content for her readers to consume, understanding others, learning new cultures, and of course, writing.